THE SELF-LOVE PATH

HOW TO EMBRACE SELF-COMPASSION AND KINDNESS TO YOURSELF AND ACHIEVE YOUR GOALS

ARIANE S. TURPIN

THE LUXE NORTH
—PUBLISHING—

Published by The Luxe North Publishing

Montreal, QC, Canada

www.arianeturpin.com

CONTENTS

Introduction   vii

1. CHAPTER 1: THE IMPORTANCE OF GOAL
   SETTING   I
   The Three Cs of Goal-Setting   2
   The Three Rs of Goal-Setting   5
   Other Goal-Setting Models   7

2. CHAPTER 2: SMART GOALS   I I
   What are SMART Goals?   I I
   Limitations of SMART Goals   20
   Strategies to Maximize the Benefits of SMART
   Goals while Mitigating their Potential Pitfalls   23
   Goal-Setting Exercises   36

3. CHAPTER 3: OVERCOMING NEGATIVE
   SELF-TALK   45
   Three Main Distortions Associated with
   Negative Self-Talk   46
   Strategies for Overcoming Negative Self-Talk   50
   Engaging in Cognitive Behavioral Therapy
   (CBT)   53
   Replace Negative Thoughts with Positive Ones   55

4. CHAPTER 4: UNDERSTANDING SELF-
   KINDNESS   57
   The Importance of Self-Kindness   57
   Debunking Myths about Self-Kindness   59

5. CHAPTER 5: SELF-COMPASSION AND YOUR
   GOALS   71
   What is Self-Compassion?   71
   Strategies to Cultivate Self-Compassion in
   Relation to Your Goals   73

6. CHAPTER 6: FOSTERING SELF-LOVE 85
   What is Self-Love? 85
   Self-Love Strategies 86
   The Strategy of Establishing Boundaries 99
   Practical Ways of Self-Love 101

7. CHAPTER 7: LEVEL UP WITH KANBAN: A
   VISUAL TOOL FOR GETTING
   THINGS DONE 111
   The Frog 113
   The Koi Fish 113
   The Woodpecker 114
   Classifying Tasks 115

8. CHAPTER 8: BUILDING RESILIENCE AND
   SELF-KINDNESS 121
   Developing Resilience Skills 122
   Overcoming Setbacks and Challenges with
   Self-Kindness 126
   Cultivating a Resilient Mindset 129

9. CHAPTER 9: SELF-REFLECTION AND
   GROWTH 133
   The Power of Self-Reflection 133
   Recognizing Areas for Personal Growth 135
   Cultivating a Growth Mindset 137
   Embracing Mistakes and Learning from
   Failure 140

   Conclusion 145
   About the Author 151
   Also by Ariane S. Turpin 153
   References 155

FREE GIFT FOR MY READERS

Just for you! Get this free ebook as my gift to you for being my valued reader. You will have access to 5 weeks' worth of journal prompts (a total of 35) which serve as your invitation to explore different aspects of your journey on the self-love path, encouraging deep self-reflection and nurturing a positive mindset.

Visit ebook.arianeturpin.com/selflovejournal or scan the above QR code.

INTRODUCTION

In a world consumed by the pursuit of outward achievements, we often neglect the most essential component of our journey: ourselves. We toil relentlessly, driven by societal expectations and the desire for success, all while our inner well-being quietly withers away.

But what if I told you that the key to true fulfillment doesn't lie in pushing harder or sacrificing more, but in cultivating self-love along the way? You most likely already had this in mind, hence why you have this book in your hands so that you can discover more and dive deeper into it. Let me assure you that you are on the right track as this book is here to be your companion on your path to self-love; for you to embrace self-compassion and kindness to yourself so that you can achieve your goals and transform how you approach your aspirations.

We will take the steps to self-discovery, exploring the connection between self-kindness, self-compassion, and the attainment of our goals. Together, we will unravel the layers of societal conditioning and reframe our understanding of ess, placing self-care and compassion at the very heart of journey.

Research studies show that individuals who possess higher levels of self-compassion tend to be more motivated, less lazy, and more successful over time (Neff, Self-Compassion.org, as cited in Pace, 2016). Additionally, they are able to maintain a positive self-regard even when they fall short. According to psychologist Susan David, cultivating self-compassion involves recognizing and acknowledging difficult thoughts and emotions, creating a sense of psychological safety, and allowing oneself to take risks and explore new possibilities. This quality enables individuals to learn from their experiences without getting caught up in blame and judgment.

To develop self-compassion, it is important to end the internal tug-of-war by refraining from black-and-white evaluations of your experiences and emotions. Rather than berating yourself for negative feelings, it is beneficial to view them as valuable data that provide insights into your personal values and priorities. By approaching difficult emotions with curiosity and asking meaningful questions, you can gain perspective and make wiser decisions aligned with your goals and values.

When struggling to access self-compassion, you can imagine connecting with the child version of yourself and responding with kindness and understanding. Ultimately, self-compassion is about embracing the realities of our humanness, including discomfort, stress, disappointment, and imperfections. Recognizing and accepting these aspects of being human allows you to navigate life with kindness and the understanding that you are doing your best with the resources available to you.

And so our journey begins in the sphere of goal setting—a foundational pillar on which our dreams and ambitions are built. However, we will go beyond mere goal setting as a checklist of accomplishments. We will delve into introspection, guiding you to discover your most authentic desires and purpose. Through exercises and insightful guidance, you will learn to create goals that are not only compelling but also deeply aligned with your values and aspirations.

And then, there's more. We will confront head-on the internal barriers that often sabotage your progress—the prevalent negative self-talk and cognitive distortions that burden your self-belief. Through self-exploration, you will become equipped and empowered with powerful strategies to challenge and transform these self-limiting beliefs. With renewed clarity and a resilient mindset, you will forge ahead, equipped to overcome obstacles and achieve noteworthy results.

Next, we jump into the sphere of self-compassion. You will discover the transformative potential of embracing your fundamental worth and treating yourself with unwavering kindness and love. You will nurture self-care, enhance resilience, and cultivate an unshakeable foundation of self-compassion on your path to goal achievement.

As our journey progresses, you will utilize a remarkable tool—the Kanban method—that will reshape your approach to productivity and handling your objectives and goals. With this transformative approach, your to-do lists become dynamic tools for unlocking possibilities, helping you prioritize tasks, streamline your workflow, and enhance your focus. This method empowers you to make meaningful progress towards your goals with efficiency and clarity.

I wrote this book because of my sincere passion to help

others. The wealth of valuable learnings and experiences I've accumulated over the years have shaped me into the person I am today. I understand the struggles and challenges that can arise when striving to achieve our goals. At times, I have been particularly hard on myself, setting high expectations and feeling overwhelmed by the weight of my ambitions.

There have been moments when the pressure to succeed caused me feelings of anxiety, discouragement, and self-doubt. I found myself questioning my abilities and feeling disheartened when things didn't go as planned. But, through self-reflection and emotional maturity, I came to realize the importance of being kind and compassionate towards myself.

At the end of the day, my goal is to help you not have to go through the same challenges and hardships that I faced. You deserve to embrace your worthiness and cultivate a sense of self-compassion. It is important to recognize that you are capable of achieving greatness and that setbacks and obstacles are a natural part of the journey.

I hope I can inspire you to approach your goals with more self-kindness through the experiences and insights that I will share. Instead of being overly critical or judgmental of yourself, I encourage you to adopt a mindset of self-compassion and understanding. A kinder approach to any obstacles that come your way is how you will find the resilience and strength to overcome these.

I am with you, through this book, so you are not alone in your pursuit of success and fulfillment. Together, we can cultivate a mindset that fosters growth, resilience, and self-acceptance. By acknowledging your worth and treating yourself with kindness, you will unlock the incredible potential within you. I know that there may be twists and turns in your personal growth journey but now you have this book as your constant companion, offering guidance, inspiration, and practical strategies to navigate these and help transform your relationship with yourself and your goals.

Remember, achieving your goals is a journey, and it's perfectly normal to encounter setbacks and challenges along the way. Rather than letting these moments define you, view them as opportunities for growth and learning. Embrace the lessons they offer and use them as stepping stones towards your ultimate vision of success.

I firmly believe that you have the power within you to accomplish remarkable things. By being compassionate towards yourself, celebrating your achievements, and learning from your failures, you will develop the resilience and determination necessary to overcome any obstacles and create a life that is aligned with your aspirations.

So, as you go on this transformative journey, I encourage you to embrace self-kindness, acknowledge your worthiness, and believe in your inherent ability to achieve greatness. You are capable, and with a compassionate mindset, you can navigate any challenges that come your way. You have the strength to thrive and create a life that brings you joy, fulfillment, and success. You can do this!

CHAPTER 1: THE IMPORTANCE OF GOAL SETTING

G oal setting is a powerful practice that provides us with a long-term vision and fuels us with short-term motivation. It enables us to assess where we currently stand in our lives while paving the way to a future we desire. Think of it as a roadmap guiding us towards our desired destination.

When we set goals, we break them down into objectives, allowing us to understand the necessary steps to be taken. By doing so, we shift from passively letting life happen to us to actively designing the life we want. Goal setting empowers you to take control of your life and shape your future according to your aspirations. What's more, it cultivates positive habits that contribute to our personal growth.

When done correctly, goal setting becomes a habit-building process. We can implement new habits on a weekly or monthly basis, gradually integrating them into our life-style. It transforms from a mundane chore to a way of life. Additionally, goal setting encourages deep reflection on our behaviors. It provides an opportunity to examine the aspects of ourselves or our unhealthy habits that we wish to change. It is essential to reflect on how our maladaptive behaviors may impact not only ourselves but also the people around us.

Consistent goal setting enhances our resiliency as individuals. As we set goals and work towards achieving them, we acquire new resources and develop new thought patterns. Whether it's obtaining a gym membership, meeting with a mentor, or engaging in therapy, we open ourselves up to a multitude of opportunities and gain valuable resources and support. This journey of personal development and growth equips us with the resilience to face challenges head-on and overcome obstacles.

Numerous models and variations of goal-setting exist, ranging from the three Cs to the three Rs of goal-setting. It can be overwhelming to navigate through these options. The key is to find a model that resonates with you and aligns with your lifestyle. Remember, the goal is not to become overwhelmed by the process. Regardless of the model you choose, they all share a common aim: helping you achieve your goals. Developing and identifying goals that suit your unique circumstances takes time and introspection. Seeking the assistance of a life coach or therapist can be immensely valuable during this process.

THE THREE CS OF GOAL-SETTING

The Three Cs of goal-setting, namely Clarity, Commitment, and Consistency, serve as pillars to guide and enhance your journey towards achieving your goals. Let's delve deeper into each of these principles and understand how they contribute to your overall success.

Clarity

Clarity is the foundation upon which effective goal-setting is built. It involves gaining a crystal-clear understanding of what you want to achieve. Clarity enables you to define your goals in a specific, measurable, achievable, relevant, and time-bound manner (SMART goals). When your goals are specific, you have a clear target to work towards, and it becomes easier to measure your progress and success. By ensuring that your goals are realistic and relevant to your aspirations and values, you align your efforts with what truly matters to you. Time-bound goals provide a sense of urgency and help you prioritize your actions. With clarity, you can chart a clear path towards your desired outcomes and stay focused on what truly matters.

Commitment

Commitment entails making a dedicated and unwavering decision to pursue your goals wholeheartedly. It is about nurturing a strong determination and resolve to do whatever it takes to accomplish what you have set out to do. Commitment requires a willingness to invest your time, effort, and resources into your goals. It means staying dedicated even when faced with challenges, setbacks, or distractions. When you are truly committed to your goals, you develop a mindset that is resilient, tenacious, and driven. This level of commitment fuels your motivation and helps you stay on track, even during difficult times. It keeps you focused on your vision and strengthens your resolve to overcome obstacles along the way.

Consistency

Consistency is the key to turning your goals into reality. It involves taking regular and persistent action towards your objectives. Consistency is about creating daily or weekly habits and routines that align with your goals. By consistently working on your goals, you build momentum and make progress, step by step. Consistency helps you avoid procrastination and keeps you from getting derailed by distractions. When you cultivate consistency, you develop a sense of discipline and follow-through that propels you forward. It helps you develop a rhythm and flow in your actions, making it easier to sustain your efforts over time. By showing up consistently, you create a solid foundation for success and ensure that each small step contributes to the larger picture.

* * *

By integrating the Three Cs of goal-setting into your approach, you empower yourself to make significant strides towards your aspirations. Clarity provides you with a clear sense of direction, guiding your actions and choices. Commitment fuels your motivation, determination, and resilience, enabling you to persevere through challenges. Consistency ensures that you maintain steady progress, staying on track and avoiding the pitfalls of procrastination or inconsistency.

It is important to remember that the Three Cs are not isolated principles but rather interconnected and mutually reinforcing. Clarity strengthens your commitment, as it is easier to stay dedicated when you have a clear understanding of what you are working towards. Commitment fuels your consistency, as your strong determination helps you stay on track and take regular action. Consistency, in turn, reinforces your clarity and commitment, as each small step forward builds confidence and reinforces your belief in the attainability of your goals.

Incorporating the Three Cs into your goal-setting process can significantly enhance your chances of success. By gaining clarity, making a deep commitment, and embracing consistency, you create a framework that supports and propels you towards the realization of your dreams.

THE THREE RS OF GOAL-SETTING

The Three Rs of goal-setting—Realistic, Relevant, and Rewarding—provide a framework for setting goals that are meaningful, attainable, and fulfilling. Let's explore each of these principles in more detail to understand their significance in the goal-setting process.

Realistic

Realistic goals are essential for setting yourself up for success. When you set realistic goals, you ensure that they are achievable and attainable based on your current circumstances, resources, and abilities. It involves considering the practical aspects of your goals, such as the time, effort, and skills required to accomplish them. Realistic goals take into account any limitations or constraints you may have and set expectations that are within your reach. By setting realistic goals, you avoid setting yourself up for disappointment or frustration. Instead, you create a foundation of confidence and motivation, as you know that the goals you have set are within your capabilities. This increases your belief in your ability to achieve them, and as a result, you are more likely to stay committed and motivated throughout the journey.

Relevant

Relevance is another important aspect of goal-setting. Relevant goals are aligned with your values, interests, and long-term objectives. They are meaningful to you and contribute to your personal or professional growth. When your goals are relevant, they resonate with your deepest desires and aspirations, giving you a sense of purpose and direction. This alignment between your goals and your values fuels your motivation and commitment. Relevant goals keep you engaged and focused because they represent what truly matters to you. They provide a clear connection between your actions and your larger vision for your life. By setting relevant goals, you ensure that your efforts are directed towards what brings you joy and a sense of fulfillment.

Rewarding

The rewarding aspect of goal-setting recognizes the benefits and rewards associated with achieving your goals. By identifying and acknowledging the positive outcomes that come with accomplishing your goals, you enhance your motivation and commitment to pursue them. Rewards can be intrinsic, such as personal satisfaction, a sense of accomplishment, or improved self-confidence. They can also be extrinsic, such as tangible rewards or recognition. By under-standing the rewards that await you, you create a sense of anticipation and excitement for the journey. The rewards serve as markers of progress and reminders of the value and impact of your efforts. They provide a sense of fulfillment and drive as you experience the positive outcomes that come with achieving your goals.

* * *

Incorporating the Three Rs into your goal-setting process helps you set meaningful and attainable objectives that align with your capabilities, values, and aspirations. Realistic goals ensure that you set yourself up for success by considering practical factors and avoiding setting unrealistic expectations. Relevant goals connect your actions to what truly matters to you, providing a sense of purpose and motivation throughout the journey. Recognizing the rewarding aspects of your goals fuels your motivation, satisfaction, and enjoyment as you work towards achieving them.

When setting goals, take the time to evaluate their realism, relevance, and potential rewards. Reflect on whether they align with your current circumstances, values, and aspirations. Consider the practicality of achieving them and the benefits they will bring to your life.

OTHER GOAL-SETTING MODELS

While the three Cs (Clarity, Commitment, and Consistency) and the three Rs (Realistic, Relevant, and Rewarding) are popular goal-setting models, here are a few additional goal-setting models that you may find helpful:

OKR Goal-Setting Model

The Objectives and Key Results model, popularized by companies like Google, focuses on setting ambitious objectives and identifying key results that measure progress towards those objectives. It emphasizes alignment and transparency within organizations.

WOOP Goal-Setting Model

WOOP (Wish, Outcome, Obstacle, Plan) is a four-step goal-setting method developed by Gabrielle Oettingen. It involves identifying a wish or goal, imagining the desired outcome, considering potential obstacles, and creating a specific plan of action to overcome those obstacles.

GROW Goal-Setting Model

The GROW model is commonly used in coaching and stands for Goal, Reality, Options (or Obstacles), and Will (or Way Forward). It helps individuals define their goals, assess their current reality, explore options and potential solutions, and create a plan of action to move forward.

Backward Goal-Setting

In this approach, you start by envisioning your desired end result, and then work backward to determine the steps needed to reach that outcome. By starting with the end in mind, you can ensure that your actions are aligned with your ultimate goal.

Power of Three

This model involves selecting three key goals or tasks to focus on at any given time. By limiting your focus to three priorities, you can avoid spreading yourself too thin and increase your chances of making significant progress in those areas.

* * *

Remember, the goal-setting model you choose should resonate with you and suit your unique circumstances. You can experiment with different models and approaches to find what works best for you. And if you feel overwhelmed or stuck, seeking the guidance of a life coach or therapist can provide valuable support and insights on your goal-setting journey.

CHAPTER 2: SMART GOALS

Now, we delve into the widely recognized and commonly used model of goal-setting known as SMART goals. While this model has its merits, we will explore its nuances and potential drawbacks. Through an examination of the SMART goal framework, we will uncover ways to refine and optimize our goal-setting process for greater effectiveness and satisfaction.

WHAT ARE SMART GOALS?

SMART is an acronym that stands for **S**pecific, **M**easurable, **A**chievable, **R**elevant, and **T**ime-Bound. Let's break down each component to gain a comprehensive understanding of this goal-setting approach.

Specific

Specificity is the cornerstone of a SMART goal. By

utilizing the five Ws (Who, What, Where, When, and Why), you would create a clear and detailed objective.

- Who is involved in this goal?
- What do I want to accomplish?
- Where can this goal be achieved?
- When do I want to achieve this goal?
- Why do I want to achieve this goal?

Let's consider **Example #1: Health and Fitness.**

Goal Statement: *I want to get into shape.*

This statement lacks specificity and provides little guidance. To transform it into a SMART goal, you would specify, "I want to obtain a gym membership at my local community center and work out four times a week to improve my overall health." The specificity clarifies the target, location, frequency, and purpose, allowing for a more precise direction.

Measurable

Measurability is the next crucial aspect of a SMART goal. It involves defining criteria to track progress and determine success. You ask yourself, "How much? How many?" In our example, we set a measurable indicator: "Every two weeks, I aim to lose one pound of body fat." This quantifiable measure provides tangible evidence of progress and allows for adjustments if necessary.

Achievable

Achievability evaluates whether a goal is realistic and within your capabilities and available resources. It is essential to consider if you possess the necessary tools, skills, and support to achieve the goal. For instance, before committing to a gym membership, you must assess your financial situation and overall readiness for such an investment. It is crucial to acknowledge that not all goals may be achievable at a particular moment, and that's perfectly acceptable. You need to be honest with yourself about your limitations and explore alternative paths or adapt your aspirations accordingly.

Relevant

Relevance examines the alignment between your goals and your broader aspirations, values, and priorities. It ensures that your goals contribute meaningfully to your personal growth and well-being. By asking yourself if the goal is relevant to your current circumstances and aspirations, you can determine if it holds significance and aligns with your overall life direction. It is vital to assess whether the goal resonates with your values and brings you closer to your desired future.

Time-Bound

Time-Bound refers to setting a specific start and finish date for your goals. It establishes a sense of urgency and creates a deadline for completion. By defining a timeframe, you enhance your focus, motivation, and commitment. For example, "I will start at the gym on July 1st. By the end of July, my goal is to have lost four pounds of body fat." This time-bound structure adds structure to your goal-setting process and enables you to track your progress more effectively.

Example #2: Advancing in Your Career

Now that we have a better understanding of what SMART goals are and how they can be applied, let's explore another example of how this framework can be utilized to advance in one's career.

> *Goal Statement: Within the next 12 months, I will secure a promotion to a leadership position in my current company.*

Specificity

In order to make the goal more specific, you need to define the leadership position you are aiming for. Let's say your target is a senior manager role within the Sales Department.

> *Revised Goal Statement: Within the next 12 months, I will secure a promotion to the senior manager position in the Sales Department of my current company.*

Measurability

To make your goal measurable, you need to establish clear criteria for success. In this case, you can define specific metrics such as revenue targets, team size, or project accomplishments that are typically associated with a senior manager role.

>*Revised Goal Statement: Within the next 12 months, I will secure a promotion to the senior manager position in the Sales Department of my current company by leading a team of at least 10 sales representatives, achieving a revenue growth of 20%, and successfully overseeing a major product launch.*

Attainability

It is crucial to ensure that your goal is realistic and attainable. You should evaluate your skills, qualifications, and experience to determine if you are currently positioned to take on a senior manager role. If there are any gaps, you can identify the necessary steps to acquire the required knowledge and expertise.

>*Revised Goal Statement: Within the next 12 months, I will secure a promotion to the senior manager position in the Sales Department of my current company by completing a leadership training program, enhancing my knowledge of sales strategies through industry certifications, and actively seeking mentorship opportunities.*

Relevance

Your goal should align with your long-term aspirations, values, and career trajectory. You need to ensure that pursuing a leadership position in the Sales Department is consistent with your overall career goals and personal ambitions.

> ***Revised Goal Statement:*** *Within the next 12 months, I will secure a promotion to the senior manager position in the Sales Department of my current company, which aligns with my long-term goal of becoming a respected leader in the field of sales and advancing my career within the organization.*

Time-bound

Setting a specific timeframe is crucial to create a sense of urgency and ensure that you stay focused on achieving your goal. You should establish milestones and checkpoints along the way to track progress and make necessary adjustments.

> ***Revised Goal Statement:*** *By December 31st of next year, I will secure a promotion to the senior manager position in the Sales Department of my current company, which aligns with my long-term goal of becoming a respected leader in the field of sales and advancing my career within the organization. I will regularly review my progress every quarter to assess my growth and make any necessary adjustments to stay on track.*

* * *

This example above illustrates how the SMART goals approach can provide focus, direction, and motivation to individuals seeking professional growth. By breaking down our objectives into specific and actionable steps, we enhance our chances of success and pave the way for a fulfilling and rewarding career journey.

Example # 3: Personal Development

Now let's explore an example of how the SMART goals framework can be applied to personal development, focusing on enhancing a specific skill or area of personal growth.

Goal Statement: Over the next six months, I will improve my public speaking skills to confidently deliver a presentation to a large audience.

Specificity

To make your goal more specific, you need to define the aspects of public speaking you want to improve and identify the target audience for your presentation. Let's say you want to work on your ability to engage the audience and deliver a clear message, and your target audience is a professional conference with at least 200 attendees.

Revised Goal Statement: Over the next six months, I will improve my public speaking skills to confidently deliver a captivating presentation to a large audience of at least 200 professionals at a professional conference.

Measurability

To make your goal measurable, you need to establish clear criteria for success. You can define specific metrics such as the level of audience engagement, positive feedback received, or the ability to deliver the presentation within a given time limit.

> *Revised Goal Statement: Over the next six months, I will improve my public speaking skills to confidently deliver a captivating 30-minute presentation to a large audience of at least 200 professionals at a professional conference, receiving positive feedback from at least 80% of the attendees.*

Attainability

You need to ensure that your goal is realistic and attainable. It's important to assess your current public speaking skills, identify areas for improvement, and develop a plan to acquire the necessary knowledge and practice to reach your target.

> *Revised Goal Statement: Over the next six months, I will improve my public speaking skills to confidently deliver a captivating 30-minute presentation to a large audience of at least 200 professionals at a professional conference by*

*attending a public speaking course, practicing
regularly with a speaking coach, and seeking
opportunities to speak in front of smaller groups
to gain confidence.*

Relevance

Your goal should align with your personal aspirations, values, and desired personal growth. You need to ensure that improving your public speaking skills is consistent with your overall personal development goals and aligns with your interests and passions.

> *Revised Goal Statement: Over the next six months,
> I will improve my public speaking skills to confi-
> dently deliver a captivating 30-minute presenta-
> tion to a large audience of at least 200
> professionals at a professional conference. This
> goal aligns with my personal aspiration to
> become a more effective communicator and
> share my expertise with a wider audience.*

Time-bound

Setting a specific timeframe is essential to create a sense of urgency and maintain focus. You should establish milestones and checkpoints along the way to track progress and make necessary adjustments.

> *Revised Goal Statement: By the end of six months
> from today, I will improve my public speaking
> skills to confidently deliver a captivating 30-*

minute presentation to a large audience of at least 200 professionals at a professional conference. I will practice regularly, attend a public speaking course, work with a speaking coach, and seek opportunities to speak in front of smaller groups to gain confidence. I will evaluate my progress every month and make adjustments to my training plan as needed.

* * *

This example above demonstrates how SMART goals can provide structure, motivation, and a clear roadmap for personal growth. By breaking down our objectives into specific and actionable steps, we increase our chances of success and open doors to personal transformation and fulfillment.

LIMITATIONS OF SMART GOALS

While the SMART goal framework can be a valuable tool for clarity and direction, it is important to acknowledge the potential limitations and drawbacks they entail. The rigidity of this model, with its emphasis on specific timelines and outcomes, may inadvertently set you up for feelings of failure or disappointment if you do not meet the predetermined criteria. Furthermore, the focus on achieving the end result often overlooks the significance of celebrating small wins along the way. Recognizing and appreciating the incremental progress you make and adjusting your goals as needed is crucial.

Rigidity and Narrow Focus

The structure of SMART goals, while providing clarity, can inadvertently create a rigid mindset that focuses solely on the specific timelines and outcomes. This narrow focus by adhering strictly to the SMART framework may hinder your ability to recognize alternative paths or adapt to changing circumstances. This rigidity can limit creativity, adaptability, and flexibility in goal pursuit. It is essential to remain open-minded and flexible in your approach to goal pursuit to embrace unforeseen opportunities and address evolving needs.

Unrealistic Expectations

Despite the emphasis on setting realistic goals, there is still a risk of setting overly ambitious expectations by some individuals, especially if they lack a thorough understanding of their capabilities and resources. If you set goals that are beyond your current capabilities or resources, you may face disappointment, frustration, and a sense of failure. It is crucial to assess your capabilities honestly and set goals that challenge you without overwhelming you.

Neglecting Non-Measurable Aspects

SMART goals primarily emphasize quantifiable outcomes, such as specific targets or metrics, potentially neglecting important non-measurable aspects of personal growth or organizational success. Keep in mind that even if personal development, relationships, creativity, and other non-measurable aspects may not be adequately addressed within the SMART framework, they are equally important. It is essential to consider and integrate these aspects into your goal-setting process to ensure a well-rounded approach to your overall development and well-being.

Lack of Contextual Considerations

While SMART goals provide a structured approach to goal setting, they may not account for the contextual factors that can influence goal achievement. External circumstances, resource availability, or unforeseen challenges can significantly impact your ability to achieve certain goals within the predefined timelines. It is important to be mindful of these contextual factors and adjust your goals accordingly to ensure they remain relevant and attainable.

Limited Emphasis on Process

SMART goals mainly focus on the desired outcomes and may not pay enough attention to the process of goal pursuit. The journey toward a goal is often as important as the end result as it is often filled with learning, growth, and self-discovery. Neglecting the process can diminish the overall satisfaction and intrinsic rewards that come from the pursuit of a goal. It is important to appreciate the progress made along the way and celebrate the small wins that contribute to your personal development.

* * *

To overcome these limitations, it is important that you adopt a more holistic and adaptable approach to goal setting. Consider incorporating additional frameworks or strategies that address the broader aspects of your growth and well-being. For example, you can complement SMART goals with practices like self-reflection, mindfulness, and regular evaluation of your priorities and values. This allows you to adjust your goals as needed and ensures that they align with your evolving aspirations and circumstances.

Remember that goal setting is not a one-size-fits-all process as sometimes, the path you envision may not align with your evolving circumstances or priorities. It is a dynamic and personal journey that requires continuous self-assessment and adaptation. By being open to re-evaluating and modifying your goals when necessary, you empower yourself to make informed decisions about when to persevere or persist and when to pivot or redirect your efforts. Embrace the flexibility to adjust your goals and embrace new opportunities that align with your evolving path.

STRATEGIES TO MAXIMIZE THE BENEFITS OF SMART GOALS WHILE MITIGATING THEIR POTENTIAL PITFALLS

While the SMART goal framework provides a structured approach to goal-setting, it is essential to employ certain strategies to maximize its benefits and mitigate the potential pitfalls that may arise along the way. By incorporating these strategies into your goal-setting process, you can enhance your chances of success, maintain motivation, and navigate any challenges that may arise. Let's explore these strategies.

1. Break Down Goals into Milestones

To avoid becoming overwhelmed by the magnitude of a goal, it is helpful to break it down into smaller, manageable milestones. By dividing the goal into achievable steps, you create a sense of progress and celebrate accomplishments along the way. Each milestone serves as a stepping stone towards the ultimate objective, keeping you motivated and focused.

Let's consider an example to illustrate the concept of breaking down goals into milestones. Suppose your goal is to start your own online business. This goal can feel daunting and overwhelming when viewed as a whole. To make it more manageable and actionable, you can break it down into milestones:

- **Milestone # 1:** Research and Planning: The first milestone could be conducting market research, identifying your target audience, and developing a business plan. This step allows you to lay the foundation for your business and gain clarity on your niche and competitive landscape.
- **Milestone # 2:** Branding and Website Development: Once you have a clear understanding of your business concept, the next milestone could be creating a brand identity and developing a professional website. This step involves designing a logo, selecting a color scheme, and creating a user-friendly website that showcases your products or services.
- **Milestone # 3:** Product or Service Development: This milestone involves developing or sourcing the

products or services you plan to offer. It may include conducting product testing, refining prototypes, or creating service packages that align with your target audience's needs.

- **Milestone # 4:** Marketing and Promotion: With your products or services ready, the next milestone could be focused on marketing and promotion. This step involves developing a marketing strategy, establishing a social media presence, and implementing various promotional activities to raise awareness and attract customers.
- **Milestone # 5:** Launching and Initial Sales: This milestone marks the official launch of your online business and the start of your initial sales. It could include setting up an online store, implementing a secure payment system, and executing your marketing strategies to drive traffic and generate sales.
- **Milestone # 6:** Growth and Expansion: Once your business is up and running, the next milestone could be focused on growth and expansion. This step may involve scaling your operations, exploring new markets or product lines, and continuously refining your marketing efforts to increase your customer base and revenue.

By breaking down your goal of starting an online business into these milestones, you create a clear roadmap and actionable steps. Each milestone represents a significant accomplishment and brings you closer to realizing your ultimate objective. This approach allows you to stay motivated, track your progress, and celebrate achievements along the way. Additionally, if you encounter challenges or need to make adjustments, it becomes easier to identify which specific milestone requires attention, rather than feeling overwhelmed by the entire goal.

2. Embrace Flexibility

While the SMART framework emphasizes specificity and measurable outcomes, it is crucial to remain flexible and adaptable. Life is filled with unexpected twists and turns, and circumstances may change. Being open to revising your goals when necessary allows you to respond to new opportunities or challenges that may arise. Flexibility enables you to make adjustments without feeling discouraged or limited by rigid timelines.

To illustrate the importance of flexibility within the SMART framework, let's consider an example. Suppose your SMART goal is to run a marathon within six months. You set a specific outcome (running a marathon), a measurable criterion (completing the race within a certain timeframe), an achievable target (based on your current fitness level and training capacity), relevant to your personal fitness aspirations, and time-bound (within six months).

However, halfway through your training, you sustain an injury that requires you to take a break from running for several weeks. This unexpected circumstance presents a challenge to your original goal timeline. Instead of becoming discouraged or pushing through the injury, you demonstrate flexibility and adaptability within the SMART framework:

- **Specific:** You re-evaluate your specific goal to consider the new circumstances. While running a marathon within the original timeline may no longer be feasible, you maintain the focus on participating in a marathon.

- **Measurable:** You adjust the measurable criterion to reflect the new circumstances. Instead of aiming for a specific timeframe, you shift the focus to completing the marathon once you have recovered from the injury.
- **Achievable:** You acknowledge that running the marathon within the original timeframe may not be achievable given the injury. However, you recognize that with proper recovery and rehabilitation, participating in a future marathon is still attainable.
- **Relevant:** The relevance of the goal remains intact, as participating in a marathon aligns with your personal fitness aspirations and reflects your commitment to an active and healthy lifestyle.
- **Time-bound:** While the original timeframe may no longer be applicable, you set a new time-bound goal of participating in a marathon once you have fully recovered and regained your fitness level.

By demonstrating flexibility and adapting your goal within the SMART framework, you allow yourself the opportunity to recover and return to training when appropriate. This approach prevents you from pushing through the injury and potentially causing further harm. It also ensures that you remain motivated and committed to your goal while acknowledging the importance of taking care of your physical well-being. By remaining open to revising your goals when necessary, you create a more realistic and sustainable path towards success.

3. Cultivate Self-Compassion

Goal pursuit can be demanding, and setbacks are inevitable. It is essential to cultivate self-compassion throughout the journey. Be kind to yourself when facing obstacles or experiencing temporary setbacks. Practice self-care, acknowledge your efforts, and focus on progress rather than perfection. Self-compassion enables resilience and promotes a healthy mindset, allowing you to bounce back and continue working towards your goals.

Imagine you have set a goal to improve your physical fitness by running a marathon. As you begin your training, you encounter various challenges along the way. One day, you experience a minor injury that forces you to take a break from running. You might feel frustrated, disappointed, or even tempted to give up on your goal.

In this situation, cultivating self-compassion becomes crucial. Instead of berating yourself for the setback, you choose to be kind and understanding. You remind yourself that setbacks are a natural part of any journey, and they do not define your worth or ability to achieve your goal. You acknowledge that your body needs time to heal and that taking care of yourself is essential. You listen to your body and give it the rest and care it needs to recover. You may seek support from a healthcare professional or engage in alternative forms of exercise that don't aggravate your injury.

In addition, you shift your focus from perfection to progress. Rather than dwelling on the fact that you couldn't run for a few days, you celebrate the progress you have made so far. You acknowledge the effort you have put into your training, the miles you have already covered, and the improvements you have noticed in your endurance and strength. By recognizing your progress, no matter how small, you build resilience and maintain a positive mindset.

4. Regularly Review and Refine Goals

Goals are not set in stone. Regularly reviewing and refining your goals is essential for maintaining alignment with your evolving priorities, values, and circumstances. As you progress on your journey, take time to assess whether your goals are still relevant and meaningful. Make necessary adjustments to ensure that your goals continue to inspire and motivate you.

Imagine you set a goal to start your own business and become financially independent. As you undertake this entrepreneurial journey, you engage in regular review and refinement of your goals.

After a few months of running your business, you notice that your initial goal of achieving financial independence solely through your business is becoming increasingly challenging. You realize that your circumstances have changed, and you now have additional responsibilities and financial obligations that require a more balanced approach.

In this situation, regularly reviewing and refining your goals becomes crucial. You take the time to assess whether your goals are still aligned with your current priorities and circumstances. You consider the challenges you have encountered and the insights you have gained during your entrepreneurial journey. Through this process, you recognize the need to refine your goals to incorporate a more balanced approach to financial independence. You may decide to explore additional income streams or adjust your timeline for achieving financial independence. You also consider the possibility of seeking financial support or partnerships to alleviate some of the burdens and challenges you are facing.

As you make these refinements, you ensure that your goals continue to inspire and motivate you. You reassess the meaning and significance of your goals in light of your evolving priorities and values. You ask yourself important questions such as, "Does this goal still align with my long-term vision?" and "Will achieving this goal bring me the fulfillment and satisfaction I desire?"

Through regular review and refinement, you create a dynamic goal-setting process that allows you to adapt to changing circumstances and maintain alignment with your aspirations. This practice enables you to stay engaged and motivated on your entrepreneurial journey. It also fosters a sense of empowerment as you take ownership of your goals and make adjustments that reflect your current reality.

5. Seek Support and Accountability

Enlist the support of others to help you stay accountable and motivated. Share your goals with trusted friends, family, or mentors who can provide encouragement and guidance along the way. Consider partnering with an accountability buddy or joining a supportive community where you can share experiences, celebrate milestones, and seek advice when needed. Having a support system can significantly increase your chances of success.

Let's return to the example of the goal to improve your

physical fitness and run a marathon. You've always admired marathon runners and want to challenge yourself to complete a race. However, you recognize that training for a marathon requires discipline, endurance, and support. To increase your chances of success, you decide to seek support and accountability from others.

First, you share your goal with your spouse or a close friend who is also passionate about fitness. You discuss your aspirations, the training plan you've researched, and your commitment to achieving your goal. Your spouse or friend offers encouragement and agrees to join you on your fitness journey. They become your accountability partner, someone who will train alongside you, hold you accountable to your training schedule, and provide motivation when needed.

Additionally, you join a local running group or an online community of marathon runners. Here, you find a community of like-minded individuals who share similar goals and experiences. The group provides a supportive environment where you can exchange training tips, share successes and challenges, and receive advice from experienced runners. Through this community, you gain a sense of camaraderie and support, knowing that others are on a similar journey.

As you begin your marathon training, you establish a regular training routine with your accountability partner. You set specific training days and times to meet and complete your workouts together. Your partner helps you stay motivated during challenging runs, provides encouragement when you feel discouraged, and celebrates milestones with you. Having someone to share the training journey with makes it more enjoyable and keeps you committed to your goal.

In addition to your accountability partner and running

community, you seek guidance from a running coach or mentor. You connect with a seasoned marathon runner who has completed multiple races and has experience coaching others. Your coach provides personalized training plans, monitors your progress, and offers valuable insights on proper running techniques, injury prevention, and nutrition. They become a source of expertise and support, helping you navigate the intricacies of marathon training.

Throughout your training, you participate in local running events or virtual races where you can connect with other runners and gain race experience. These events allow you to assess your progress, challenge yourself in a competitive environment, and celebrate smaller achievements along the way.

By seeking support and accountability from your partner, running community, and coach, you create a network of individuals who share your passion for running and understand the challenges of marathon training. Their support, guidance, and encouragement help you stay motivated, overcome obstacles, and ultimately achieve your goal of running a marathon.

6. Celebrate Small Wins

Celebrating small victories is an integral part of the goal-setting journey. Recognize and acknowledge your progress, no matter how small it may seem. Take time to reflect on your accomplishments and reward yourself for reaching milestones along the way. Celebrating small wins boosts motivation, reinforces positive habits, and fuels your momentum towards achieving more significant goals.

Let's return to the example of setting a goal to improve

your physical fitness and lead a healthier lifestyle. You start by committing to a regular exercise routine and making healthier food choices. As you progress on your fitness journey, you actively celebrate small wins to keep yourself motivated and on track. After a few weeks of consistent effort, you notice that you have successfully established a habit of going to the gym three times a week. This is a significant achievement for you, as it required overcoming initial resistance and making exercise a regular part of your routine. To celebrate this small win, you decide to treat yourself to a relaxing spa day as a reward for your dedication and progress.

As you continue on your fitness journey, you achieve another small win - you manage to run a mile without stopping for the first time in years. This accomplishment makes you feel proud of your progress and boosts your confidence in your physical abilities. To celebrate this milestone, you plan a fun day out with friends, engaging in outdoor activities and enjoying a healthy picnic together.

By celebrating these small wins, you reinforce positive habits and maintain your motivation to pursue your fitness goals. Each celebration serves as positive feedback, signaling to your brain that your efforts are paying off and that you are making progress towards your desired outcome.

In addition, celebrating small wins helps you stay committed to your goal and fuels your momentum. It creates a positive cycle of achievement and celebration, where each small win becomes a stepping stone towards more significant accomplishments. It also provides you with a sense of satisfaction and fulfillment. As you see the results of your efforts, you become more driven to continue making healthier choices and working towards your ultimate fitness objectives.

Remember that the rewards don't have to be extravagant or costly. The key is to find meaningful ways to acknowledge your progress and achievements. It could be as simple as treating yourself to your favorite healthy meal, spending quality time with loved ones, or taking time to engage in a hobby you enjoy.

7. Maintain Balance and Self-Care

Remember that goal-setting is not solely about achieving external outcomes but also nurturing your well-being and maintaining balance in your life. Prioritize self-care, ensuring that your physical, emotional, and mental health are nurtured throughout the process. Set realistic expectations and avoid overloading yourself with too many goals. Strive for a harmonious integration of goal pursuit and self-nurturing practices to sustain long-term success.

First and foremost, prioritize your physical health. Engage in regular exercise that aligns with your capabilities and preferences. Whether it's going for a run, practicing yoga, or participating in a team sport, physical activity not only promotes physical well-being but also releases endorphins, boosting your mood and energy levels. Make time for proper nutrition, ensuring that you nourish your body with wholesome foods that provide the necessary nutrients and energy for optimal performance. Prioritize sufficient sleep, as a well-rested mind and body are better equipped to handle challenges and make progress towards your goals. Even taking a relaxing bath will allow yourself moments of rest and rejuvenation, as periods of relaxation and downtime are essential for replenishing your energy and maintaining a healthy balance.

Equally important is nurturing your emotional and mental well-being. Incorporate practices that support your emotional health in your daily routine, such as mindfulness meditation, journaling, or engaging in hobbies that bring you joy and relaxation like reading a book or hiking in nature. Cultivate self-awareness by regularly checking in with your emotions and thoughts, allowing yourself to process and release any stress or negativity. Seek support from trusted friends, family members, or a therapist when needed, as they can provide a listening ear, guidance, and valuable insights.

Remember to set realistic expectations for yourself and your goals. While ambition and drive are admirable, it's crucial to recognize your limitations and avoid overloading yourself with too many goals at once. By setting realistic expectations, you can create a balanced approach that takes into account your other commitments, responsibilities, and personal needs. Assess your capacity and prioritize the goals that truly align with your values and aspirations. Embrace the concept of "good enough" and be gentle with yourself, understanding that progress is more important than perfection.

By implementing these above strategies, you can harness the power of SMART goals while navigating the potential challenges and setbacks that may arise. Stay flexible, compassionate towards yourself, and focused on the journey of growth and self-improvement. With a mindful and strategic approach, you can maximize the benefits of

SMART goals and create a path towards personal fulfillment and success.

GOAL-SETTING EXERCISES

In the next few pages are exercises to help you create compelling and aligned goals. You can write down your responses on the pages; or if you are reading this as an ebook, grab a notebook to write down your responses.

Exercise # 1: Reflect on Your Values

Take some time to reflect on your core values. What principles and beliefs are most important to you? Write down a list of your top values, such as honesty, creativity, or adventure.

Exercise # 2: Goal-Values Alignment

Create a list of your current goals and compare them to your list of core values. Evaluate your goals: Are they aligned with your values or are there any conflicts and realignments needed? If you find any discrepancies, take some time to reconsider and redefine those goals to ensure they are in harmony with what you hold dear.

Exercise # 3: Visualize Your Ideal Future

C lose your eyes and imagine your ideal future. Envision yourself in the next five or ten years, living a life that is fulfilling and meaningful to you. What do you see? What goals have you achieved? Take some time to write a detailed description of this ideal future, capturing all the aspects that are important to you, such as career, relationships, personal growth, and lifestyle. You can use this visualization as inspiration for creating compelling goals that will lead you towards that future.

Exercise # 4: Identify Your Passions and Interests

Think about the activities and pursuits that bring you joy and ignite your passion. What are you naturally drawn to? Write down a list of your passions and interests, whether it's painting, gardening, writing, or playing a musical instrument. Consider how you can incorporate these passions into your goals. By aligning your goals with your passions, you increase your motivation and enjoyment along the journey.

Exercise # 5: Set SMART Goals

U se the SMART goal framework to create clear and actionable goals. This exercise helps you establish goals that are focused, attainable, and aligned with what you truly desire. Write down a list of goals that include each of the corresponding components.

- Specific
- Measurable
- Achievable
- Relevant
- Time-bound

Exercise # 6: Seek External Input

R each out to a trusted friend, mentor, or coach and share your goals with them. Seek their insights and perspective on whether your goals are compelling and aligned with your values. Sometimes an outside perspective can provide valuable feedback and help you refine your goals further. Embrace the support and guidance of others as you navigate the process of creating meaningful and aligned goals. Identify and write down who these people are that you will be reaching out to.

* * *

Remember that goal setting is not a one-time activity but an ongoing process. Schedule regular check-ins with yourself to review your goals and assess their alignment with your values and aspirations. Make adjustments as needed to ensure that your goals continue to inspire and motivate you. This practice of regular reflection and adjustment allows you to stay connected to your goals and make any necessary course corrections along the way.

Through these above exercises, you are on the path of creating goals that are not only compelling but also deeply aligned with your values and aspirations. By aligning your goals with what truly matters to you, you can experience a sense of fulfillment and purpose as you work towards their achievement.

CHAPTER 3: OVERCOMING NEGATIVE SELF-TALK

Negative self-talk can be a significant obstacle to achieving your goals and can even exacerbate feelings of anxiety and depression. It is the inner dialogue that diminishes your progress and undermines your belief in your abilities. When you constantly hear negative messages, whether from others or yourself, you begin to internalize them and doubt your potential. Overcoming negative self-talk is essential for fostering self-confidence and maintaining motivation on your goal-setting journey.

Be mindful of the difference between self-reflection and negative self-talk. While self-reflection allows you to evaluate your actions and make necessary adjustments, negative self-talk is destructive and demotivating. It tells you that you are inadequate or incapable of success, leading you to question whether you should even try. Recognizing this distinction is crucial for fostering a positive mindset.

Negative self-talk can be influenced by various cognitive distortions that shape our perception of ourselves and the world around us. These distortions can lead to self-limiting beliefs, reduced self-esteem, and increased anxiety, so it is important to understand what they are in order that we can challenge them and cultivate a more positive and realistic mindset.

THREE MAIN DISTORTIONS ASSOCIATED WITH NEGATIVE SELF-TALK

Personalizing

Personalizing is a cognitive distortion in which you automatically blame yourself when something negative occurs. It involves assuming responsibility for events or situations that may be beyond your control or influenced by various factors. For example, if a friend cancels plans, a person engaging in personalizing may immediately think, "They canceled because they don't like me." It can have a detrimental impact on your self-kindness and well-being.

This distortion tends to disregard other possible explanations and unnecessarily burdens us with unwarranted self-blame. You would automatically blame yourself for negative events or situations, even when the responsibility may lie elsewhere or factors beyond your control are at play. You assume that you are the cause of the problem or that the negative outcome is a reflection of your worth or likability.

Recognizing personalizing allows you to challenge the assumption that you are always at fault and encourages you to consciously shift to a more balanced and objective perspective. When you catch yourself personalizing, take a moment to evaluate the evidence supporting your assumption. Ask yourself if there are any alternative explanations for the situation.

For the example of the friend who canceled their plans on you, remind yourself that there could be various reasons unrelated to you, such as their own personal issues, schedule conflicts, or unforeseen circumstances. Consider the broader context and gather all available information before jumping to conclusions.

Disqualifying the Positive

Disqualifying the positive is a cognitive distortion that involves dismissing or discounting positive aspects of a situation or comment, focusing only on the negative. This often stems from low self-esteem or a negative self-image. It can lead to a skewed perception of reality, where achievements, compliments, or positive experiences are overlooked or diminished. It involves downplaying or disregarding positive feedback, accomplishments, or favorable events, while disproportionately focusing on the negative aspects.

For instance, if someone receives praise for their work but brushes it off as insignificant or believes it was only luck, they are disqualifying the positive. This kind of distortion undermines your self-worth and prevents you from fully appreciating and internalizing positive experiences.

By consciously acknowledging and giving credit to positive aspects, you can counteract this distortion and foster a more balanced and appreciative mindset. Instead of brushing off the praise, accept it graciously and genuinely by saying thank you. Take it to heart and acknowledge your strengths and the efforts you made. Allow yourself to bask in the positivity of the moment and recognize that you deserve to receive recognition and appreciation.

Catastrophizing

Catastrophizing is a cognitive distortion characterized by magnifying and exaggerating the potential negative outcomes of a situation. It involves envisioning the worst-case scenario, even when evidence or likelihood suggests otherwise. For instance, if a person makes a small mistake at work, they may catastrophize by thinking, "I'm going to get fired, and my career will be ruined." This distortion amplifies anxiety and stress, often leading to excessive worry and unnecessary distress.

Catastrophizing can significantly impact your well-being and mental state since with this distortion, you would tend to blow things out of proportion and imagine the worst possible outcomes, even when there is little evidence to support such catastrophic predictions. It can create a cycle of anxiety, fear, and distress, making it challenging to approach situations with a clear and calm mindset.

By challenging catastrophizing thoughts and considering more realistic and balanced perspectives, you can reduce anxiety and approach situations with greater calm and clarity.

To counter the habit of catastrophizing and cultivate self-kindness, the first step is to become aware of when you engage in this distortion. In this case, for the example stated, recognize that the catastrophizing thought is the belief that making a small mistake will lead to being fired and a ruined career.

Notice the thoughts and language you use when faced

with challenging situations. Pay attention to any tendency to immediately jump to the worst-case scenario or imagine exaggerated negative outcomes. Take a moment to ask yourself if there is any concrete evidence or factual basis for the catastrophic outcome you are envisioning. Often, you will find that the likelihood of the worst-case scenario is minimal or even improbable.

Try reframing the situation in a more positive or realistic light. Consider the potential opportunities for growth, learning, or resilience that may arise from the situation. Look for constructive solutions or alternative perspectives that can help you navigate the challenges with a more optimistic mindset. In this case, acknowledge that making small mistakes is a normal part of learning and growth in any job. Remind yourself that one mistake does not define your entire career, and it is unlikely to have such severe consequences.

Ask yourself if there are other possible outcomes that are more realistic. Consider the likelihood of less extreme consequences, such as receiving feedback or an opportunity to learn from the mistake. Remember that mistakes are opportunities for growth and improvement.

Seeking the perspective of others would also be helpful. Talk to a trusted colleague, supervisor, or mentor about the situation. Share your concerns and and ask if they can provide a more objective view about it. Most likely they would reassure you that the consequences of the mistake are not as severe as you may have initially thought.

Finally, shift your focus from dwelling on the mistake to finding constructive solutions. Take proactive steps to rectify the error, such as discussing it with your supervisor, seeking guidance, or implementing measures to prevent similar mistakes in the future. By taking action, you regain a sense of control and actively address the situation.

* * *

Recognizing and understanding these cognitive distortions is the first step toward managing negative self-talk. By becoming aware of our tendencies to personalize, disqualify the positive, or catastrophize, we can actively challenge these distortions and replace them with more balanced and empowering thoughts. With practice and self-compassion, we can cultivate a positive and realistic mindset that promotes our well-being and supports our personal growth.

STRATEGIES FOR OVERCOMING NEGATIVE SELF-TALK

To combat negative self-talk, you can employ various strategies.

1. Start with Positive Affirmations

Begin each day with a set of positive affirmations tailored to your goals and aspirations. By affirming your strengths and capabilities, you counteract the tendency to blame yourself when faced with challenges or setbacks.

2. Focus on the Positive

Disqualifying the positive is a cognitive distortion that causes us to overlook or discount positive aspects of a situation or feedback. Combat this by creating a list of your achievements and strengths. Remind yourself of your abilities and accomplishments, emphasizing the positives in your life and work.

3. Challenge Catastrophic Thinking

Catastrophizing involves magnifying potential negative outcomes and dwelling on worst-case scenarios. Develop a set of universal questions to challenge your automatic negative thoughts. By examining what you can control, identifying positives, and acknowledging what is beyond your control, you can counteract catastrophic thinking and shift your perspective.

4. Give Your Inner Critic a Name

By recognizing and labeling your inner critic, you can separate it from your true self. Understand that these negative thoughts are not valid assessments of your worth or abilities. Viewing them as separate entities allows you to distance yourself from their influence.

5. Engage in Cognitive Behavioral Therapy (CBT)

Therapy can be a powerful tool for identifying and challenging core beliefs that contribute to negative self-talk. Working with a therapist trained in CBT techniques can help you develop healthier thought patterns and build resilience.

6. Practice Gratitude

Incorporate gratitude into your daily routine as a means of empowering yourself. Recognize and appreciate the positive aspects of your life, fostering a sense of perspective and optimism. Gratitude can counteract negative self-talk by shifting your focus towards what you have rather than what you lack.

7. Utilize Coping Strategies

Explore coping strategies such as meditation, journaling, or listening to podcasts that provide psychoeducation. These techniques can help you manage stress, enhance self-awareness, and develop a more positive and compassionate mindset.

8. Replace Negative Thoughts with Positive Ones

Practice turning negative thoughts into positive ones. Whenever you catch yourself engaging in negative self-talk, consciously challenge and reframe those thoughts with more empowering and optimistic alternatives. This habit, derived from cognitive behavioral therapy, can gradually reshape your inner dialogue.

9. Seek Practice and Persistence

Overcoming negative self-talk requires consistent effort and practice. Treat it like learning a musical instrument— regular practice is essential. Be patient with yourself and persevere in reducing negative self-talk by consciously implementing positive self-talk. It may take time, but with dedication, you can transform your inner dialogue and foster a healthier mindset.

* * *

By implementing these strategies, you can gradually overcome negative self-talk and create a more empowering and supportive internal dialogue. Remember, practice is key, and embracing a positive mindset is a transformative journey that can enhance your overall well-being and propel you towards achieving your goals.

ENGAGING IN COGNITIVE BEHAVIORAL THERAPY (CBT)

Let's talk more about engaging in Cognitive Behavioral Therapy (CBT). CBT can be a life-changing step in addressing negative self-talk and improving your mental well-being. It is a widely recognized and effective therapeutic approach that focuses on the connection between thoughts, feelings, and behaviors. By working with a trained therapist, you can gain valuable insights into your core beliefs and thought patterns that contribute to negative self-talk.

A CBT therapist will guide you through the process of identifying and challenging these negative core beliefs. They will help you explore the evidence supporting or contradicting these beliefs and assist you in developing alternative, more realistic and positive perspectives. Through guided exercises and discussions, you can uncover the underlying assumptions and cognitive distortions that fuel negative self-talk.

Therapy sessions will provide a safe and supportive environment for you to express your thoughts and emotions openly. Your therapist will help you develop strategies and coping mechanisms to effectively manage negative self-talk and replace it with healthier, more empowering thoughts. Over time, you will learn to recognize when negative self-talk arises and actively challenge it, fostering a more positive and balanced mindset.

One of the great benefits of CBT is its emphasis on practical techniques and skills that you can apply outside of therapy sessions. Your therapist may provide you with homework assignments, such as keeping thought records or engaging in specific behavioral exercises, to reinforce the therapeutic work. These tools empower you to continue the progress made in therapy and build resilience in your day-to-day life.

It's important to note that CBT is a collaborative process. Your active participation and willingness to engage in introspection and practice new skills are vital for achieving lasting change. The therapeutic relationship between you and your CBT therapist is based on trust, mutual respect, and a shared commitment to your well-being.

While therapy can be a transformative tool, it's important to remember that progress takes time. CBT is typically conducted over a series of sessions, allowing for gradual exploration and change. Each individual's journey is unique, and the pace of therapy will be tailored to your specific needs and goals.

By engaging in CBT, you are investing in your mental health and well-being. Through the guidance and support of a trained therapist, you can develop healthier thought patterns, challenge negative self-talk, and cultivate a more positive and resilient mindset that extends beyond the therapy room.

REPLACE NEGATIVE THOUGHTS WITH POSITIVE ONES

Here's an example of how to turn a negative thought into a positive one. Let's say you find yourself ruminating and catastrophizing, thinking that if you miss your bus to work, you'll get fired, won't be able to afford your house, and won't have enough to eat. Instead of dwelling on these negative thoughts, try shifting your perspective.

First, recognize that missing the bus is not the end of the world. There are alternative ways to get to work, such as reaching out to your boss to inform them you might be late or asking a coworker to fill you in on anything important. By reframing the situation, you're acknowledging that there are solutions and options available.

To help with this process, consider keeping a thought record. Write down the negative thoughts you're experiencing and then challenge them with alternative explanations. Reflect on how these thoughts make you feel emotionally and how they influence your behavior.

Remember, it's important to cultivate alternative explanations and flip the narrative. By doing so, you become an observer of your thoughts rather than getting caught in a single storyline.

CHAPTER 4: UNDERSTANDING SELF-KINDNESS

P art of the self-love path is embracing kindness to yourself. To love yourself means being kind to yourself, so let's dive deeper into understanding what that means. Self-kindness refers to the act of treating yourself with gentleness, warmth, and understanding. It involves extending the same kindness and compassion towards yourself as you would towards a close friend or loved one. Self-kindness involves being supportive, nurturing, and forgiving towards yourself, especially during challenging or difficult times. It emphasizes offering yourself comfort, care, and encouragement.

THE IMPORTANCE OF SELF-KINDNESS

Self-kindness is a fundamental aspect of nurturing a healthy and balanced life. It involves treating yourself with compassion, understanding, and gentleness, fostering a positive and supportive relationship with yourself. In today's fast-paced and demanding world, where external expectations and pressures can be overwhelming, practicing self-kindness is of utmost importance for our overall well-being and happiness.

Self-kindness is important as it relates to self-acceptance and self-love. When you practice kindness towards yourself, you acknowledge and honor your inherent worth and value as a human being. Instead of berating yourself for your flaws, mistakes, or shortcomings, self-kindness allows you to embrace your imperfections with love and understanding.

Self-kindness also plays a vital role in managing stress and promoting resilience. Life can be challenging, and we all face setbacks, disappointments, and difficult circumstances. During these times, self-kindness acts as a buffer, offering solace and comfort. It allows you to be gentle with yourself, recognizing that you are doing the best you can in any given situation. By practicing self-kindness, you alleviate unnecessary self-imposed pressure and create space for healing, growth, and renewal.

Additionally, self-kindness contributes to your mental and emotional well-being. The way you treat yourself internally has a profound impact on your thoughts, emotions, and overall mindset. When you engage in self-critical or self-judgmental thinking, you reinforce negative beliefs and limit your potential. On the other hand, self-kindness nurtures a positive and supportive inner dialogue. By monitoring your self-talk and replacing self-criticism with kind and encouraging affirmations, you foster a healthy and empowering mindset that promotes self-confidence and resilience.

Self-kindness is also closely linked to physical health. Taking care of your body with kindness and compassion allows you to establish healthy habits and prioritize self-care. It involves listening to your body's needs and responding to them with love and attention. Whether it's nourishing your-self with nutritious food, getting enough rest, engaging in regular physical activity, or seeking appropriate medical care, self-kindness serves as a guiding principle for making choices that support your physical well-being.

Furthermore, self-kindness enhances your relationships with others. When you practice kindness towards yourself, you become more attuned to your own needs and emotions. This self-awareness enables you to communicate and connect with others from a place of authenticity and empa-thy. By modeling self-kindness, you can inspire and encourage others to cultivate the same attitude towards themselves, fostering a culture of compassion and under-standing.

DEBUNKING MYTHS ABOUT SELF-KINDNESS

Despite the numerous benefits and importance of self-kind-ness, there are several myths and misconceptions that can hinder individuals from fully embracing this practice. Let's explore some common myths surrounding self-kindness:

Myth #1: Self-Kindness is Self-Indulgence

Self-kindness may be misconceived to be the same as self-indulgence. However, self-kindness is not about exces-sive self-focus or prioritizing your own needs at the expense of others. It is about finding a balance between self-care and caring for others, recognizing that nurturing yourself allows you to show up more fully and authentically in your rela-tionships and responsibilities.

Let's take this example of Mandy. Mandy is a dedicated

caregiver for her elderly parents. She spends most of her time taking care of their needs, managing their medical appointments, and ensuring they have everything they require. Mandy rarely takes time for herself and often feels exhausted and overwhelmed.

In this scenario, Mandy believes that taking care of herself would be selfish or indulgent. She fears that if she prioritizes her own well-being, she may be neglecting her responsibilities towards her parents. This belief is based on the misconception that self-kindness is equivalent to self-indulgence.

However, Mandy's lack of self-kindness begins to take a toll on her mental, emotional, and physical health. She starts feeling burned out, resentful, and unable to provide the level of care she desires for her parents. Mandy realizes that neglecting her own needs actually hinders her ability to care for others effectively.

With a shift in perspective, Mandy starts to understand that self-kindness is not selfish; it is essential for her overall well-being and the quality of care she provides. She recognizes that she deserves love, compassion, and self-care, just as much as her parents do.

Mandy starts implementing small acts of self-kindness. She sets boundaries by scheduling regular breaks for herself, during which she engages in activities that bring her joy and relaxation. She attends a yoga class twice a week, meets up with friends for a coffee, or takes a leisurely walk in nature. These self-care activities rejuvenate her and allow her to recharge.

As Mandy practices self-kindness, she realizes that it benefits not only herself but also her parents. She becomes more patient, compassionate, and present during their interactions. Mandy notices that by taking care of her own needs, she has more energy, empathy, and resilience to offer her parents.

Through Mandy's example, you can see that self-kindness is not self-indulgence or selfishness. It is an essential aspect of maintaining overall well-being and being able to show up for others effectively. By recognizing and honoring your own needs, you enhance your ability to care for others and lead a more balanced and fulfilling life. Self-kindness is not about neglecting your responsibilities but about finding a healthy equilibrium that allows you to nurture yourself and others with love, compassion, and authenticity.

Myth #2: Self-Kindness is Weakness

Some people perceive self-kindness as a sign of weakness or vulnerability. They believe that being tough on themselves and pushing through difficulties is a more admirable approach. However, self-kindness is not a sign of weakness but a display of strength and resilience. It takes courage to acknowledge your limitations, embrace your vulnerabilities, and treat yourself with compassion in the face of challenges.

Let's talk about the example of Carter. Carter, a high-achieving project manager, has always prided himself on his strong work ethic and determination. He believes that self-kindness is a sign of weakness and that pushing himself relentlessly is the key to success. Carter constantly sets high standards for himself and is critical of any perceived short-comings.

One day, Carter faces a major setback at work. Despite his best efforts, a project he was leading doesn't meet the expected outcomes, and he feels a sense of disappointment and self-blame. In the past, Carter would have berated himself for the failure, viewing it as a personal reflection of his abilities.

However, this time, Carter decides to approach the situation differently. He takes a step back and recognizes the damaging effects of his self-critical mindset. He realizes that constantly pushing himself without offering self-kindness is not sustainable and often leads to burnout and decreased motivation.

With this newfound awareness, Carter decides to practice self-kindness. Instead of berating himself for the setback, he acknowledges that mistakes happen and that he is only human. He reminds himself that setbacks are opportunities for growth and learning. Carter takes the time to reflect on what went wrong. Now, he focuses on the lessons learned and the steps he can take to improve in the future instead of dwelling on his mistakes.

As Carter embraces self-kindness, he begins to notice positive changes in his overall well-being and performance. He finds that treating himself with compassion and understanding actually boosts his motivation, resilience, and problem-solving skills. By embracing self-kindness, Carter is better equipped to bounce back from challenges and adapt to new situations.

In Carter's example, you can see that self-kindness is not a sign of weakness, but rather a demonstration of strength and resilience. By acknowledging your vulnerabilities and treating yourself with compassion, you create a supportive and empowering mindset. Self-kindness allows you to bounce back from setbacks, learn from your mistakes, and ultimately achieve greater success and well-being. It takes courage to be kind to yourself and embrace your humanity, and in doing so, you cultivate a foundation of strength and resilience in all areas of your life.

Myth #3: Self-Kindness is Selfish

Another misconception is that prioritizing self-kindness is selfish and takes away from others. However, self-kindness is not about neglecting your responsibilities or disregarding the needs of others. It is about recognizing your own worth and well-being, which enables you to show up for others with greater empathy, compassion, and authenticity.

Meet Shelly, a devoted mother of two young children. Shelly has always put her family's needs before her own, believing that prioritizing herself would be selfish. She constantly finds herself exhausted, overwhelmed, and feeling guilty whenever she takes a moment for self-care.

One day, Shelly reaches a breaking point. She realizes that she can't continue giving her best to her family if she neglects her own well-being. She understands that self-kindness is not selfish but essential for her overall happiness and ability to care for others effectively.

Shelly decides to carve out small pockets of time for self-care each day. She starts waking up 30 minutes earlier to enjoy a cup of tea and engage in some quiet meditation, journaling, or reading. She also joins a local pilates class once a week, which allows her to unwind and recharge, and she joins a book club which meets once a month. Initially, she feels a twinge of guilt for taking time away from her family, but she soon realizes that her self-care practices positively impact her mood, energy levels, and ability to be present for her loved ones.

As Shelly continues to prioritize self-kindness, she

notices a significant shift in her relationships and interactions with her family. She is more patient, understanding, and emotionally available. By taking care of her own well-being, she has more to give to her children and spouse.

Shelly's journey exemplifies how self-kindness is not selfish but an essential aspect of being able to care for others. When we neglect our own needs, we may become resentful, burnt out, and less capable of providing the support and love that others require. By prioritizing self-kindness, we are better equipped to nurture healthy relationships, maintain our emotional well-being, and be a positive presence in the lives of those around us.

In Shelly's example, you can see that self-kindness is not about neglecting others or being selfish. It is about recognizing the importance of your own well-being and how it positively impacts your ability to care for and support others. When you prioritize self-kindness, you create a healthier and more balanced dynamic in your relationships, allowing you to show up with genuine empathy, compassion, and love.

Myth #4: Self-Kindness is a Luxury

Some people view self-kindness as a luxury that can only be afforded by those with ample time, resources, or privilege. However, self-kindness is a basic human need that is essential for overall well-being. It does not require extravagant gestures or expensive indulgences. Simple acts of self-care, self-compassion, and self-acceptance can go a long way in nurturing your inner self.

Now, let's meet Max. Max is a hardworking college student who is juggling multiple part-time jobs to support themselves financially. They often feel overwhelmed and exhausted due to the demands of their busy schedule. Max has always believed that self-kindness is a luxury they cannot afford, as their time and energy are dedicated to meeting their responsibilities and obligations.

One day, Max's close friend Jen notices their exhaustion and encourages them to prioritize self-kindness, even in small ways. She suggests that Max takes short breaks throughout the day to engage in activities that bring them joy and rejuvenation. Despite feeling skeptical at first, Max decides to give it a try.

During their study breaks, Max takes a walk in nature, listens to their favorite music, or practices deep breathing exercises. These moments of self-care provide a much-needed respite from their hectic routine. They notice that even these brief moments of self-kindness help replenish their energy, reduce stress, and improve their focus when they return to their tasks.

Over time, Max realizes that self-kindness is not a luxury but a necessity for their well-being. They come to understand that taking care of themselves allows them to be more productive and effective in their work. They start incorporating self-kindness practices into their daily routine, such as prioritizing sleep, eating nourishing meals, and setting boundaries to prevent burnout.

By embracing self-kindness, Max experiences a positive shift in their overall well-being. They feel more balanced, happier, and better equipped to handle the challenges that come their way. Max's example demonstrates that self-kindness does not require extravagant resources or excessive time commitments. It can be woven into our daily lives through simple acts of self-care, self-compassion, and self-acceptance.

In Max's example, you can see that self-kindness is not a luxury reserved for a privileged few. It is a fundamental aspect of well-being that everyone deserves, regardless of their circumstances. By recognizing the importance of self-kindness and incorporating it into their lives, Max discovers that small acts of self-care can have a significant positive impact on their overall happiness and ability to navigate life's challenges.

Myth #5: Self-Kindness Means Always Being Positive

Self-kindness does not mean ignoring or suppressing negative emotions or experiences. It is not about perpetually maintaining a positive outlook or denying the challenges you face. Self-kindness involves acknowledging and accepting your whole range of emotions and experiences with compassion and understanding. It is about offering yourself support and comfort during difficult times and learning from those experiences to grow and thrive.

Now, let me share Tammy's story. Tammy is a young professional who recently experienced a setback in her career. She had been working diligently towards a promotion but was unexpectedly passed over for the opportunity. Tammy felt a mix of disappointment, frustration, and self-doubt in the aftermath of this news.

In the past, Tammy believed that self-kindness meant always being positive and suppressing any negative emotions. She would dismiss her disappointments and put on a brave face, trying to convince herself that everything was fine. However, this approach only intensified her feelings of frustration and prevented her from truly processing the situation.

This time, Tammy decided to approach the situation with self-kindness and self-compassion. Instead of denying her emotions, she allowed herself to feel the disappointment and acknowledged that it was a normal reaction to an unexpected outcome. Tammy recognized that self-kindness did not require her to put on a façade of positivity but rather to offer herself support and understanding in moments of difficulty.

Tammy reached out to a close friend and shared her feelings about the setback. Her friend listened without judgment and provided a safe space for Tammy to express her emotions. Through this conversation, Tammy gained perspective and realized that she had been placing too much of her self-worth on external validation.

Instead of berating herself for not achieving the promotion, Tammy practiced self-kindness by reframing the situation. She acknowledged her hard work and the progress she had made, recognizing that this setback was an opportunity for growth and self-reflection. Tammy chose to focus on the lessons she could learn from the experience rather than dwelling on self-criticism.

In the following weeks, Tammy engaged in self-reflection and identified areas for personal and professional development. She took the setback as motivation to improve her skills and expand her knowledge. Tammy signed up for additional training courses and sought mentorship to support her growth. Through this process, she developed a deeper sense of self-compassion and understood that setbacks were not a reflection of her worth but rather a part of her learning journey.

Tammy's example demonstrates that self-kindness is not about suppressing negative emotions or maintaining a constant state of positivity. It is about allowing yourself to feel and acknowledging the full range of emotions that arise in challenging situations. By offering yourself support, understanding, and acceptance during difficult times, you can cultivate resilience and learn valuable lessons that contribute to your personal growth and well-being. Self-kindness encourages you to embrace your experiences, both positive and negative, with compassion and use them as stepping stones towards self-improvement.

Myth #6: Self-Kindness Equals Self-Criticism

Some individuals mistakenly believe that self-kindness requires being overly critical and demanding of oneself to achieve personal growth or success. However, self-kindness rejects harsh self-criticism as a motivator and instead encourages self-compassion and gentle self-improvement. It involves treating yourself with understanding, forgiveness, and patience, while still striving for personal growth and development.

Let's take the example of Dana. Dana is a student who has always held herself to incredibly high standards. She believed that in order to succeed, she needed to constantly criticize and push herself to her limits. Dana would often set unrealistic expectations and harshly judge herself for any perceived shortcomings.

One day, Dana found herself overwhelmed and burnt out. She realized that her approach of self-criticism was not sustainable and was taking a toll on her mental and emotional well-being. It was at this point that she decided to embrace self-kindness as an alternative approach.

Instead of constantly criticizing herself for not meeting impossibly high standards, Dana began practicing self-compassion. She acknowledged her limitations and accepted that making mistakes was a natural part of the learning process. Dana started treating herself with understanding and forgiveness, replacing self-criticism with self-encouragement.

To implement this change, Dana set realistic and achievable goals for her academic pursuits. She learned to celebrate her accomplishments, big or small, without dismissing them as insignificant. When faced with challenges or setbacks, Dana responded with self-compassion, offering herself support and encouragement to keep going.

Rather than viewing mistakes as failures, Dana recognized them as opportunities for growth. She approached her studies with curiosity and a willingness to learn from her experiences. This shift in perspective allowed her to embrace a mindset of continuous improvement, free from the burden of self-criticism.

As a result of practicing self-kindness, Dana noticed positive changes in her overall well-being. She felt more motivated, resilient, and at peace with herself. The shift from self-criticism to self-compassion enabled her to cultivate a healthier relationship with herself and her goals.

Dana's example highlights how self-kindness is not about equating personal growth with self-criticism. Instead, it emphasizes the importance of treating yourself with compassion, understanding, and patience. By embracing self-kindness, individuals like Dana can foster a positive and supportive inner dialogue, allowing for personal growth and development without sacrificing their mental and emotional well-being.

* * *

I t is important to recognize and challenge these myths surrounding self-kindness. By debunking these misconceptions, we can fully embrace the practice of self-kindness and experience its transformative effects on our well-being and overall quality of life.

CHAPTER 5: SELF-COMPASSION AND YOUR GOALS

I n this chapter, let's uncover how self-compassion relates to goal-setting. Some people worry that being lenient, kind, and gentle towards themselves will make them lazy and self-indulgent, leading to a loss of motivation. However, similar to self-kindness as discussed earlier, this is a misconception as self-compassion does not equate to self-indulgence. Self-compassion is not about being easy on yourself; it is a way of nurturing yourself to reach your full potential.

WHAT IS SELF-COMPASSION?

Self-compassion is the act of directing kindness inward, replacing judgment with understanding. It involves acknowledging that suffering and feelings of inadequacy are common to everyone, and it requires you to be attentive and mindful of your emotions.

Self-compassion encompasses a broader concept that includes self-kindness but also involves two other key elements: common humanity and mindfulness. In addition to being kind to yourself, self-compassion involves recognizing and acknowledging that suffering, imperfection, and difficulties are part of the shared human experience. It cultivates a sense of interconnectedness and understanding that others also face challenges. Mindfulness, another aspect of self-compassion, involves being aware and present in the moment without judgment, allowing yourself to fully experience and accept emotions and thoughts without resistance or self-criticism.

We must recognize that a lack of self-compassion can stem from various factors, including childhood stressors. While it is important not to excessively dwell on our past experiences and their impact on us, it is our responsibility to reflect on how those experiences have shaped us. In a society that often equates being hard on oneself with success and encourages us to constantly strive for the next best thing, it is important to understand the concept of "enoughness."

Enoughness enables you to honor who you are, acknowledge your personal growth, achievements, and the impact you have made. It allows you to be content in the present moment. To develop and strengthen your psychological flexibility, you need to cultivate certain practices:

Psychological Flexibility

Psychological flexibility involves being present, clarifying our values in relation to our goals, and living in alignment with those values. It means seeing ourselves as observers, acknowledging the different aspects of our lives. By unhooking from difficult thought processes and accepting things as they are, we enhance our psychological flexibility. Understanding our values and core beliefs, which can be achieved through therapy or coaching, is crucial for increasing psychological flexibility.

Creating a Safe Space

Having self-compassionate goals creates a safe space for us to effectively manage setbacks and adapt to changes. It is not about going easy on ourselves or being seen as weak. Rather, it provides a nurturing environment where we can regroup and refocus on our goals. Self-compassion turns inward, replacing judgment with kindness. It reminds us that suffering and feelings of inadequacy are part of the shared human experience and encourages us to be mindful of our emotions.

STRATEGIES TO CULTIVATE SELF-COMPASSION IN RELATION TO YOUR GOALS

Now, let's explore some strategies to cultivate self-compassion in relation to your goals.

1. Dropping Words with Baggage

When setting goals, you should be mindful of the words you use. For example, seeing words like "diet" or "exercise" may trigger negative associations due to past negative experiences. It is important to recognize how your past experiences can impact your perception of the future. By choosing words that are genuine and meaningful to you, you can avoid negative associations and feelings of defeat.

Another example of dropping words with baggage is related to personal relationships. Let's say you aim to improve your communication skills in your romantic relationship. However, in the past, you may have had negative experiences or conflicts that have left you feeling insecure or hesitant to express yourself openly.

When choosing the words associated with this goal, it's essential to be mindful of any negative associations or triggers that may arise. For instance, if the word "confrontation" or "conflict" brings up feelings of fear or anxiety, it may hinder your progress in improving your communication skills.

In this case, cultivating self-compassion involves reframing your goal and choosing words that create a safe and positive environment for growth. Instead of focusing on words that imply conflict, you could use words like "effective communication," "empathy," or "building connection." These words emphasize the intention of fostering understanding and connection in your relationship rather than dwelling on the negative aspects.

By consciously selecting words that resonate positively with you, you create a supportive and empowering mindset that encourages self-compassion. This shift allows you to approach your goal with a compassionate attitude toward yourself and your partner, promoting open and healthy communication while respecting your own emotional well-being.

Remember, the goal is to choose words that align with your values, promote growth, and eliminate negative associations from past experiences. By doing so, you create a nurturing environment that encourages self-compassion and sets the stage for meaningful progress in achieving your relationship goals.

2. Reminding Yourself of Common Humanity

It is important to understand and remind yourself that everyone faces struggles and challenges in their pursuit of goals. Comparing yourself to others can be detrimental, as they may have overcome numerous hurdles to reach their current stage, while you may be at the beginning of your journey. Recognizing the universal nature of struggle helps put your own experiences into perspective.

An example of this is in the context of career development. Let's say you have set a goal to advance in your career and secure a promotion. As you observe your colleagues or peers who have already achieved similar milestones, it's natural to compare yourself and potentially feel discouraged if you perceive yourself as lagging behind.

In such situations, it's important to remind yourself of the common humanity shared by all individuals striving for career growth. Recognize that everyone faces their own unique challenges and setbacks along the way. Some may have had more opportunities, resources, or support that have facilitated their progress, while others may have encountered obstacles that slowed them down.

By acknowledging the universal nature of struggle and understanding that everyone's journey is unique, you can shift your perspective from comparison and self-judgment to self-compassion. Instead of criticizing yourself for not being at the same level as others, remind yourself that you are on your own path, and your progress should be measured based on your personal circumstances and growth.

Furthermore, embracing the idea of common humanity allows you to view the achievements of others as sources of inspiration and learning rather than sources of self-doubt.

Instead of seeing their success as a reflection of your inadequacy, see it as evidence that your goal is attainable with time, effort, and self-compassion.

Practice self-kindness by acknowledging your progress, celebrating your achievements, and embracing the learning opportunities that challenges provide. Remember that everyone has their own unique journey, and comparing yourself to others only hinders your self-compassion and growth.

By reminding yourself of common humanity, you cultivate a mindset that fosters self-compassion, resilience, and the understanding that progress is a personal and individualized process. This shift in perspective allows you to approach your career goals with greater self-acceptance, patience, and motivation to keep moving forward on your own path of growth and development.

3. Celebrating Progress

While self-discipline is important, celebrating your progress and even your attempts can be motivating. By acknowledging and appreciating the efforts you put into your goals, you cultivate a positive mindset and the drive to continue moving forward.

Let's say you have set a goal to improve your physical fitness and incorporate regular exercise into your routine. In the beginning, you may find it challenging to establish a consistent workout schedule, and you might struggle with maintaining motivation.

To cultivate self-compassion and celebrate progress in relation to this goal, it's essential to acknowledge and appreciate even the smallest efforts and achievements along the way. For example, let's say you commit to going for a 15-minute walk three times a week as a starting point.

As you complete your first week of consistent walks, take a moment to celebrate and recognize your progress. Instead of dismissing it as insignificant or not "enough," remind yourself that you followed through on your commitment and took steps toward improving your fitness. Recognize the effort, dedication, and self-discipline it took to prioritize your health and well-being.

Consider celebrating your progress by rewarding yourself with something meaningful and aligned with your goals. It could be treating yourself to a relaxing bath, enjoying a nutritious meal, or indulging in a hobby or activity you love. The key is to choose a reward that reinforces your positive behavior and reinforces the idea that self-compassion and self-celebration are essential components of your journey.

Additionally, you can keep a progress journal or create a visual tracker to document your achievements and milestones. This tangible representation of your progress serves as a reminder of how far you've come and can be a powerful motivator during challenging times. Seeing the checkmarks or milestones reached can boost your self-confidence, fuel your determination, and inspire you to keep going.

By celebrating your progress, no matter how small, you cultivate a positive mindset and reinforce the idea that your efforts matter. You shift your focus from perfection or end results to the journey itself and the growth you experience along the way. This self-compassionate approach encourages self-acceptance, resilience, and a sustainable motivation to continue working towards your goals.

Remember, self-compassion is not about downplaying your accomplishments or waiting for significant milestones to celebrate. It is about recognizing that every step forward, no matter how small, is worthy of acknowledgment and celebration. By embracing this strategy, you foster a supportive and empowering relationship with yourself, which fuels your motivation and strengthens your commitment to personal growth and success.

4. Allowing Time for Grieving Mistakes

It is essential to allocate a specific amount of time to reflect on your mistakes or failed attempts. Normalizing mistakes and viewing relapses as part of the goal-setting process allows you to learn from them and bounce back with new and redefined goals. This reflective period is crucial for personal growth.

Let's say you have set a goal to start a side business and become an entrepreneur. You invest time, effort, and resources into launching your business, but unfortunately, it doesn't succeed as expected. You may feel disappointed, frustrated, and even blame yourself for the perceived failure.

To cultivate self-compassion and allow time for grieving mistakes in relation to your goal of entrepreneurship, it's important to recognize that setbacks and failures are a natural part of the journey. Instead of immediately berating yourself or dwelling on self-criticism, give yourself permission to grieve and process the disappointment.

Give yourself some time, which could be a day, a week, or however long a period of time it will take for you to reflect on various aspects. Think and reflect, "What went wrong, what could have been done differently, and what lessons can I learn from this experience?" During this allocated period of reflection, you can do activities that promote self-care and self-reflection, such as journaling, meditation, or seeking support from trusted friends or mentors.

Allowing yourself this dedicated time for grieving mistakes helps you normalize the experience and view it as an opportunity for growth and learning. It acknowledges that setbacks and failures are not indicators of your worth or capabilities but rather stepping stones towards success.

Once you have gone through the grieving process, it's important to shift your focus towards the lessons learned and the opportunities for growth. Use this reflective period to identify the skills and knowledge you have gained, the insights you have gained about yourself and your goals, and the adjustments you can make moving forward.

For example, you may realize that you underestimated the market demand for your product or that your marketing strategies need improvement. Instead of dwelling on the failure, approach it with curiosity and a growth mindset. Consider how you can refine your business idea, seek additional training or support, or pivot your approach to better align with your target audience.

By allowing time for grieving mistakes, you give yourself the space and compassion to process setbacks and failures, learn from them, and emerge stronger and wiser. This self-compassionate approach helps you build resilience, adaptability, and a positive mindset that propels you forward on your goal-setting journey.

Remember, mistakes and failures are not indicators of your worth or potential. They are opportunities for growth and self-discovery. Embracing self-compassion in the face of setbacks allows you to navigate challenges with resilience, learn from your experiences, and continue pursuing your goals with renewed determination and wisdom.

5. Adopting a Growth Mindset

Operating from a growth mindset involves identifying your mistakes, understanding negative patterns or processes, and seeking alternative paths. Embracing a mindset focused on learning and continuous improvement enables you to adjust your strategies and approach, leading to more effective goal pursuit.

Let's say you are starting a business, and dealing with new clients is something you would for sure expect you'd need to do. You know you're an introvert so you have set a goal to improve your public speaking skills, so you start attending workshops and practicing in front of others. For example, if you stumble over your words during a presentation, you can choose to view it as a chance to identify areas for improvement and refine your speaking skills. Rather than berating yourself for the mistake, you can adopt a curious and proactive approach.

You may reflect on what contributed to the stumble, such as nervousness or lack of preparation, and explore strategies to address those factors. This might involve seeking guidance from a speaking coach, practicing relaxation techniques to manage nerves, or rehearsing your presentations more diligently.

Instead of viewing mistakes or challenges as indicators of your inherent abilities or limitations, a growth mindset encourages you to see them as opportunities for learning and development. You recognize that skills can be developed and improved over time through effort, practice, and a willingness to learn from setbacks. The focus is shifted from self-judgment and self-criticism to a mindset centered on learning and progress. You understand that setbacks and mistakes are part of the journey towards mastery and that embracing them with self-compassion allows you to grow and develop.

In addition to seeking opportunities for improvement, a growth mindset also encourages you to celebrate small wins and milestones along the way. This recognition of progress, no matter how small, reinforces your motivation and self-belief, creating a positive cycle of learning and growth.

Remember, you cultivate self-compassion by acknowledging that improvement takes time, effort, and perseverance. You give yourself permission to make mistakes, learn from them, and continually refine your strategies and approach. This mindset shift fosters resilience, adaptability, and a sense of empowerment as you navigate the challenges and obstacles on your goal-setting journey.

6. Valuing the Intention and Process

Recognizing that the intention to pursue a goal is a form of success is important. Shifting your focus from solely outcome-oriented thinking to appreciating the efforts and progress made along the way helps you cultivate self-compassion. By rewarding yourself for making attempts and celebrating the journey, you foster a positive and nurturing mindset.

Let's say your goal is to write a novel (something I can closely relate to, although I do not have the intention to write fiction in the foreseeable future at this time). As you embark on this creative journey, it's essential to value the intention and process of writing, rather than solely fixating on the final outcome of having a published book. Cultivating self-compassion in relation to this goal involves recognizing and appreciating the efforts and progress you make along the way.

In the early stages of writing, you may face challenges such as self-doubt, writer's block, or criticism of your work. During these moments, valuing the intention and process allows you to acknowledge that simply committing to the act of writing and dedicating time and effort to your craft is a significant accomplishment in itself.

For example, even if you encounter a day where you struggle to produce the desired number of words or feel uncertain about the direction of your story, you can still celebrate the fact that you showed up and engaged in the creative process. Recognize that writing involves vulnerability and perseverance, and by honoring your commitment to the craft, you are already succeeding in nurturing your creativity and pursuing your goal.

By valuing the intention and process, you shift your focus from solely seeking external validation or approval to finding fulfillment and satisfaction in the act of creation. You allow yourself to be present in the journey, enjoying the moments of inspiration, the breakthroughs, and even the challenges that help you grow as a writer.

Additionally, celebrating the small victories and milestones along the way becomes a crucial part of cultivating self-compassion. For instance, you can acknowledge and reward yourself for completing a challenging chapter, reaching a word count milestone, or receiving positive feedback from a trusted writing partner or mentor. These acknowledgments serve as reminders that progress is happening, and they fuel your motivation and self-belief.

By valuing the intention and process, you foster a positive and nurturing mindset that supports your creative endeavors. You recognize that the path to achieving your goal is not always linear or without obstacles, but that each step, each word written, and each moment of dedication contributes to your growth and development as a writer.

Now let's consider a fitness goal as another example. Your goal is to improve your overall fitness and incorporate regular exercise into your routine.

Instead of solely focusing on achieving a specific body weight or reaching a certain level of fitness, you shift your attention to the intention behind your goal—to prioritize your health and well-being. Recognize that the act of committing to a fitness routine and prioritizing self-care is a significant achievement in itself.

For example, let's say you have a busy schedule and find it challenging to make time for exercise every day. Instead of beating up yourself for missed workouts or not meeting your expectations, value the intention and effort you put into carving out time for physical activity. Celebrate the fact that you made the conscious decision to prioritize your health and took steps towards incorporating exercise into your life.

Additionally, appreciate the process of exercise and the benefits it brings beyond just physical changes. Notice how it boosts your energy levels, improves your mood, and enhances your overall well-being. By focusing on the positive effects of exercise on your mental and emotional state, you reinforce the value of the process itself.

Furthermore, valuing the intention and process involves recognizing the small victories and progress you make along the way. Celebrate milestones such as completing a challenging workout, increasing the duration or intensity of your exercises, or mastering a new fitness skill. These acknowledgments help you build confidence, stay motivated, and reinforce the positive changes you are making in your life.

In this example, you cultivate self-compassion by embracing the journey of improving your fitness and taking care of your body and overall well-being. You acknowledge that progress is not always linear, and there may be setbacks or obstacles along the way. However, each effort you put into exercising, each healthy choice you make, and each step towards a stronger and healthier body is worth celebrating. You allow yourself to nurture the mindset that supports your long-term commitment to a healthy and active lifestyle.

Self-compassion is about appreciating and honoring your efforts, regardless of the final outcome. It fosters a sense of fulfillment, joy, and self-acceptance as you pursue your goals.

In life, we cannot avoid failure, so we need to always remember that failure is an opportunity for learning and growth. By practicing self-compassion and implementing the strategies we've discussed in this chapter, you can create a supportive and nurturing environment to manage setbacks, adapt to changes, and foster personal development. Embracing a growth mindset and recognizing your own worth and progress empower you on your goal-setting journey. As the saying goes, "Failure is not only inevitable, but also our best teacher and experience to be explored rather than avoided."

CHAPTER 6: FOSTERING SELF-LOVE

WHAT IS SELF-LOVE?

S elf-love is the deep appreciation, acceptance, and nurturing of yourself. It involves having a positive and compassionate relationship with yourself, both mentally and emotionally. Self-love encompasses acknowledging your worth, recognizing and honoring your needs, and treating yourself with kindness, care, and respect. It involves cultivating a sense of self-compassion, forgiveness, and understanding, allowing yourself to prioritize personal well-being, happiness, and growth.

Self-love is about recognizing that you are deserving of love, kindness, and fulfillment, and actively engaging in practices that promote self-care and self-empowerment. It is a journey of self-discovery, self-acceptance, and self-empowerment that plays a role in your overall well-being and personal development.

SELF-LOVE STRATEGIES

To foster self-love and create a supportive environment, there are several ways to go about it.

1. Understanding that self-care is a responsibility

By focusing on self-care and recognizing it as a responsibility, you take charge of what you put into your body, what you expose yourself to, and how you spend your time. Taking care of yourself becomes a crucial aspect of fostering self-love, as it directly impacts your ability to achieve your goals and continue setting new ones.

Lots of people work demanding jobs that require long hours and high levels of stress. I find that there are people who may often find themselves neglecting self-care in the pursuit of career success, or if not that, are just plainly over-worked. If you are in this situation, you need to acknowledge and come to the realization that self-care is not just a luxury or a treat but a responsibility that you owe to yourself.

Recognizing self-care as a responsibility means understanding that taking care of your physical, mental, and emotional well-being is essential so you can function every day as a normal human being and be able to succeed in all areas of life. It's not only about pampering or spoiling yourself; it's about making sure you have the necessary energy and resources to tackle challenges and achieve your goals.

You can start prioritizing regular exercise to keep your body strong and healthy. You can carve out time in your schedule for physical activity, whether it's going to the gym, practicing yoga, or taking a brisk walk during your lunch break. By doing so, you're fulfilling your responsibility to maintain your physical well-being, which enhances your energy levels, focus, and productivity in the workplace.

Additionally, you recognize the importance of setting boundaries and managing stress to protect your mental and emotional health. You establish clear work-life boundaries, such as avoiding work emails after a certain hour or taking breaks throughout the day to recharge. By prioritizing self-care in this way, you're fulfilling your responsibility to nurture your mental and emotional well-being, allowing you to show up as your best self in both your personal and professional life.

Understanding self-care as a responsibility also involves making conscious choices about what you expose yourself to. This may mean limiting your consumption of negative news or social media, surrounding yourself with positive and supportive people, and engaging in activities that bring you joy and fulfillment. By actively curating your environment, you're taking responsibility for your emotional well-being and creating a space that fosters self-love and positivity.

2. Inner dialogue awareness

Another important step is to be aware of your inner dialogue and the dialogue of those around you. We all have an inner critic, and it's essential to identify and label it. Recognizing when you engage in cognitive distortions or negative self-talk allows you to challenge and reframe those thoughts. Additionally, paying attention to the conversations and interactions we have with others is vital. The people you surround yourself with greatly influence your self-perception and how you present yourself to the world.

For example, let's say you're working on a project at

work, and you encounter a setback. Your immediate thought might be, "I'm such a failure. I can't do anything right." This negative self-talk undermines your confidence and erodes your self-esteem. However, with inner dialogue awareness, you catch yourself in the act of self-criticism. You pause and acknowledge that this is your inner critic speaking.

Instead of allowing the negative self-talk to spiral, you choose to challenge and reframe the thought. You remind yourself that setbacks are a natural part of the learning process and do not define your worth or abilities. You reframe the thought by saying, "This setback doesn't mean I'm a failure. It's an opportunity for growth and learning. I've overcome challenges before, and I can do it again."

By actively engaging in this process of recognizing and reframing your inner dialogue, you gradually shift your self-perception and cultivate self-love. You become more compassionate and understanding towards yourself, offering words of encouragement and support rather than criticism and self-doubt.

Additionally, inner dialogue awareness extends beyond your own self-talk to the conversations and interactions you have with others. It's important to be mindful of the dialogue happening in your external environment and its impact on your self-perception. Surrounding yourself with positive and supportive individuals who uplift and inspire you is crucial for fostering self-love.

For instance, let's say you have a friend who consistently belittles your accomplishments or dismisses your goals. Their negative dialogue and constant criticism can chip away at your self-esteem and hinder your self-love journey. By being aware of the impact of their words on your well-being, you can make a conscious choice to distance yourself from such individuals and seek out relationships that nurture and support your growth.

On the flip side, surrounding yourself with friends, mentors, or support groups who encourage and celebrate your achievements can greatly enhance your self-love. Engaging in conversations that promote positivity, growth, and self-acceptance can inspire you to embrace your worth and pursue your goals with confidence.

By cultivating inner dialogue awareness, both in your self-talk and external interactions, you empower yourself to challenge negative thoughts, reframe them with self-compassion, and create an environment that fosters self-love. This heightened awareness allows you to navigate through life with a stronger sense of self-worth and a deeper connection to your authentic self.

3. Practicing self-acceptance is key

There is no "ideal" self to strive for or a final destination where you have achieved perfection. Embracing self-acceptance means understanding that the journey itself is valuable and that there will be ups and downs along the way. Sometimes you may even take steps backward, and that's perfectly okay. It's about learning and growing through the experiences you encounter, your strengths, weaknesses, imperfections, and past mistakes.

It involves recognizing that you are a unique individual with your own set of qualities and experiences. Rather than striving for an unrealistic ideal or constantly comparing yourself to others, self-acceptance encourages you to appreciate and value who you are in the present moment.

For example, if you have the tendency to be self-critical

about your physical appearance, you may often find yourself comparing your body to societal beauty standards and feeling inadequate.

In this situation, practicing self-acceptance means acknowledging that your worth goes far beyond your physical external appearance. It involves recognizing that beauty comes in diverse forms and that everyone has unique features that make them attractive in their own way. Instead of constantly berating yourself for not fitting into a particular mold, you choose to embrace and celebrate your individuality.

By practicing self-acceptance, you shift your focus from striving for an unattainable ideal to nurturing a healthy relationship with yourself. You appreciate the strengths and qualities that make you who you are, whether it's your kindness, creativity, intelligence, or any other positive trait. You also acknowledge and accept your areas of growth and imperfections, understanding that they are part of being human.

Self-acceptance allows you to let go of self-judgment and self-criticism. It frees you from the burden of constantly seeking validation and approval from others. Instead, you find validation and fulfillment from within, recognizing your inherent worth and embracing yourself as a work in progress.

Moreover, practicing self-acceptance extends beyond your perceived flaws and encompasses accepting your past mistakes and failures. It involves understanding that mistakes are opportunities for growth and learning, not reflections of your worth or competence. By accepting your past, you release yourself from the shackles of regret and self-blame, allowing room for personal growth and trans-formation.

You need to live authentically and wholeheartedly, knowing that you are worthy of love and belonging just as you are.

4. Choosing the things you are exposed to

In today's digital age, we are constantly bombarded with information and content through various platforms, particularly social media, so being mindful of what you expose yourself to is important. You have the power to choose what you engage with.

The content you consume can have a great impact on your mental and emotional well-being, shaping your self-perception and influencing how you view yourself and the world around you. If certain content consistently harms your well-being or self-esteem, it's essential to distance yourself from it.

Instead, you can seek out positive resources, follow pages that promote positivity, and move away from content that reinforces societal expectations. Taking control of your social media consumption can significantly impact your mental health.

For example, let's say you notice that scrolling through Instagram or Facebook leaves you feeling inadequate, anxious, or discontented. You find yourself constantly comparing your life, appearance, or achievements to those portrayed by others. This constant comparison can take a toll on your self-esteem and overall well-being.

To address this, you must make a conscious decision to

choose the things you are exposed to on social media. You can start by unfollowing accounts or pages that consistently trigger negative emotions or perpetuate unrealistic standards. Instead, you can actively seek out content that promotes self-love, body positivity, personal growth, and mental health awareness.

By taking control of your social media consumption, you create a digital environment that aligns with your values and supports your journey toward self-love. You may choose to follow accounts that share empowering messages, uplifting quotes, or inspirational stories. You may engage with communities that foster a sense of belonging and provide a safe space for vulnerability and self-expression.

In addition to curating your social media feed, you might also limit the amount of time you spend on these platforms. Setting boundaries around your online engagement can help prevent comparison and negative self-talk from creeping into your mind. By consciously allocating time for activities that nourish your well-being, such as hobbies, self-care practices, or spending time with loved ones, you create a balanced lifestyle that extends beyond the digital realm.

Choosing the things you are exposed to goes beyond social media. It also involves being mindful of the books, movies, television shows, and news outlets you engage with. By being selective in what you consume, you protect yourself from unnecessary negativity, unrealistic expectations, or harmful messages that can undermine your self-love journey.

Ultimately, the power to choose what you expose yourself to empowers you to shape your inner narrative and cultivate self-love.

5. Establishing boundaries

Implementing boundaries is another valuable practice for fostering self-love. There are various types of boundaries you can establish, both within yourself and with others. Understanding the different boundary types can help you protect your own peace and well-being. Boundaries allow you to set limits on what you're comfortable with and ensure that your needs are met in your relationships and daily interactions. Say "no" when you need to and assertively communicate your needs and limits. Respecting your own boundaries shows self-respect and protects your well-being.

One example of establishing boundaries can be seen in personal relationships, whether it's with friends, family, romantic partners, or colleagues. Let's consider a scenario where you often find yourself overwhelmed and emotionally drained due to constantly saying "yes" to others' requests, even when it comes at the expense of your own well-being.

In this situation, you recognize the need to establish boundaries to protect your mental and emotional health. You begin by reflecting on your values, needs, and limits. You identify what is important to you, what energizes you, and what drains you. With this self-awareness, you start to set boundaries by clearly communicating your limits, expectations, and preferences to others.

For instance, you may inform your friends that you need one evening a week to recharge and have dedicated time for self-care. You express that while you value your friendships, it is important for you to have this time to focus on your well-being. By asserting this boundary, you communicate that you are prioritizing self-love and self-care without jeopardizing the connection and support you have with your friends.

Similarly, in a professional setting, you may establish

boundaries by clearly communicating your workload capacity and the need for a balanced work-life integration. This may involve setting realistic deadlines, delegating tasks when appropriate, and saying "no" when you are overwhelmed or when a request goes against your values or personal boundaries.

By setting boundaries, you reinforce your self-respect and assert your needs. It allows you to create healthy and balanced relationships where your well-being is prioritized. It also sends a powerful message to others that you value yourself and expect to be treated with respect and consideration.

Establishing boundaries not only benefits you but also promotes healthier dynamics in your relationships. It encourages open communication, fosters mutual respect, and prevents resentment or burnout from building up. Boundaries provide a framework for maintaining your energy, protecting your time, and nurturing your self-love.

Remember, setting boundaries is an ongoing practice that requires self-awareness and assertiveness. It may feel uncomfortable initially, but with time and practice, it becomes easier and more natural.

6. Engaging in CFT, AFT, and mindfulness

If you have the tendency to struggle with self-criticism and negative self-talk, you might find it challenging to accept your imperfections. You may also have the tendency to frequently feel overwhelmed by feelings of shame and self-doubt. In this case, engaging in CFT, ACT, and mindfulness can be transformative.

Compassion-focused therapy (CFT) is a therapeutic

approach that is particularly helpful for individuals struggling with shame and self-criticism. CFT aims to create a balance between kindness, self-criticism, and motivation, promoting emotional well-being and self-acceptance. Through various techniques and exercises, you learn to respond to yourself with kindness and understanding, fostering a nurturing and compassionate harmonious relationship with yourself.

Acceptance and commitment therapy (ACT) is another approach that can support the cultivation of self-love. ACT emphasizes accepting your thoughts and emotions, while also committing to actions aligned with your values. By embracing all aspects of yourself, including imperfections and vulnerabilities, using mindfulness skills, you allow yourself to move towards self-acceptance and personal growth. ACT helps individuals develop psychological flexibility and the ability to live in the present moment, which can enhance self-compassion and well-being.

Mindfulness practices are integral to both CFT and ACT, as well as standalone self-love strategies. Mindfulness practices equip you with techniques to approach your goals from a calm and focused state by intentionally paying attention to the present moment without judgment. It allows you to observe your thoughts, feelings, and sensations with acceptance and curiosity. You allow a deeper understanding of yourself and your experiences when you develop a nonjudgmental awareness, leading to increased self-compassion and self-acceptance.

By engaging in CFT, ACT, and mindfulness, you would gradually transform your inner dialogue and relationship with yourself. These would aid in your ability to approach your goals and challenges from a calm and focused state.

Remember that engaging in these therapeutic approaches and mindfulness practices can be done with the support of a qualified therapist or through self-guided resources.

7. Creating, not just consuming

Lastly, it's essential to focus not just on consumption but also on creation. Engaging in learning, whether through online videos such as YouTube, LinkedIn Learning, or other educational resources, and pursuing creative endeavors can enhance your sense of self-love and emotional well-being. While you have the choice to expose yourself to certain content on social media, it's equally important to consider what you can actively contribute and create.

Creating involves actively engaging in activities that allow you to express yourself, explore your interests, and contribute something meaningful to the world. It can take various forms, such as writing, painting, playing a musical instrument, cooking, crafting, or even starting a blog or a YouTube channel. Engaging in these creative endeavors nurtures your sense of self-love and emotional well-being in several ways.

Firstly, creating allows you to tap into your unique talents, passions, and interests. When you engage in activities that align with your authentic self, you experience a sense of fulfillment and self-expression. It enables you to connect with your inner desires and values, fostering a deeper under-standing and acceptance of yourself. By dedicating time and effort to something you love, you validate your own worth and creativity.

Secondly, creating promotes a sense of autonomy and empowerment. When you actively participate in the creative process, you take ownership of your ideas, decisions, and outcomes. You become the driver of your own self-expression, free from external expectations or judgments. This autonomy reinforces your sense of self and instills a belief in your ability to create and shape your own reality.

Furthermore, the act of creation offers a sense of accomplishment and growth. As you engage in creative activities, you challenge yourself, learn new skills, and overcome obstacles. Each small achievement or improvement along the way boosts your self-esteem and confidence. It reminds you that you are capable of growth and progress, which is essential for nurturing self-love and personal development.

Let's consider an example to illustrate the impact of creating, not just consuming, on cultivating self-love. Let's say you spend a significant amount of time scrolling through social media, constantly comparing yourself to others and feeling inadequate. You consume an abundance of content, but it leaves you feeling empty and disconnected from your own passions and interests.

You would need to recognize the need to shift your focus, and make the decision to allocate dedicated time to pursue a creative endeavor. If you have always had a passion for writing, you can start a personal blog where you can share your thoughts, experiences, and insights. Through writing, you can express your authentic self, explore your interests, and connect with others who resonate with your words.

As you immerse yourself in the creative process, you will find newfound sense of fulfillment and self-discovery. You would be able to tap into your creativity, develop your writing skills, and receive positive feedback from readers who find value in your work. By actively creating, this enables you to shift your attention from comparison and self-doubt to self-expression and growth.

Engaging in this creative endeavor allows you to cultivate self-love in several ways. You would gain a deeper under-standing of your own thoughts and emotions, fostering self-acceptance and self-compassion. You can find your unique voice and recognize the value you bring to others through your writing, which helps enhance your self-esteem and sense of purpose. What's more, wouldn't you agree that this would bring you joy and satisfaction when you are able to pursue your passion and contributing something meaningful to the world?

By actively creating instead of solely consuming, this allows you to break free from the cycle of comparison and external validation, focusing instead on self-expression, growth, and personal fulfillment.

Remember, whether it's writing, painting, playing an instrument, or any other creative pursuit, creating offers a powerful avenue for self-love and personal growth. By embracing the process of creation, you can nurture your authentic self, celebrate your accomplishments, and contribute something meaningful to the world around you.

* * *

By implementing these above strategies, you can foster an environment that supports self-love, empowers you to prioritize self-care, enhances your overall well-being, and create a positive relationship with yourself. Remember, fostering self-love is an ongoing process, and it requires effort and self-reflection.

THE STRATEGY OF ESTABLISHING BOUNDARIES

When it comes to fostering self-love, implementing boundaries is an important aspect of creating a supportive environment. Boundaries help you establish and maintain healthy relationships with yourself and others. There are several types of boundaries that you can implement to cultivate self-love. Let's explore these seven types:

1. Physical Boundaries

Physical boundaries involve defining and respecting personal space, touch, and privacy. It's crucial to communicate and assert your comfort levels when it comes to physical contact and personal boundaries. Setting physical boundaries allows you to prioritize your well-being and create a sense of safety.

2. Emotional Boundaries

Emotional boundaries pertain to protecting your emotional well-being. They involve setting limits on the kind of emotional energy you allow into your life and being mindful of your own emotions. It's important to recognize and communicate your emotional needs and boundaries to ensure healthy relationships and self-care.

3. Time Boundaries

Time boundaries involve managing and protecting your time. This includes setting aside dedicated time for self-care, hobbies, rest, and relaxation. By establishing boundaries around how you spend your time, you prioritize your own needs and prevent burnout or overwhelm.

4. Social Boundaries

Social boundaries revolve around choosing the social interactions you engage in and the people you surround yourself with. It's crucial to evaluate the impact of relationships on your self-esteem and well-being. Setting social boundaries allows you to foster connections that are supportive, respectful, and aligned with your values.

5. Material Boundaries

Material boundaries involve setting limits around material possessions, finances, and resources. This means being mindful of how you spend money, lend or borrow belongings, and engage in material exchanges. Establishing material boundaries helps you maintain a healthy relationship with material possessions and cultivate a sense of abundance.

6. Intellectual Boundaries

Intellectual boundaries involve respecting and valuing your thoughts, opinions, and intellectual autonomy. It means being able to express yourself freely and assertively, while also respecting the viewpoints of others. Setting intellectual boundaries allows you to engage in constructive discussions, maintain personal integrity, and protect your intellectual well-being.

7. Digital Boundaries

In our digital age, digital boundaries have become increasingly important. These boundaries involve managing your online presence, social media usage, and digital interactions. It includes being mindful of the content you consume, the platforms you engage with, and the boundaries you set around your online presence. Digital boundaries help you maintain a healthy relationship with technology and protect your mental and emotional well-being.

* * *

Implementing these various types of boundaries empowers you to prioritize self-love and self-care. Boundaries provide a framework for healthy relationships with yourself and others. They enable you to establish clear limits, communicate your needs, and create an environment that fosters self-love, respect, and well-being. Remember, boundary-setting is a personal and ongoing process, and it's important to regularly assess and adjust your boundaries as needed.

PRACTICAL WAYS OF SELF-LOVE

Self-love is a powerful practice that involves nurturing and caring for yourself, both mentally and physically. Here are some practical examples of self-love that you can incorporate into your daily life.

Prioritizing Self-Care

Make self-care a non-negotiable part of your routine. Dedicate time each day to engage in activities that bring you joy and relaxation, such as taking a warm bath, reading a book, going for a walk in nature, practicing meditation or mindfulness, or indulging in a hobby you love. Prioritize quality sleep, take breaks when needed, and engage in activities that help you unwind and recharge, such as practicing deep breathing exercises, listening to calming music, or engaging in gentle stretching or yoga.

Nourishing Your Body

Take care of your physical well-being by nourishing your body with nutritious foods, staying hydrated, and engaging in regular physical activity that you enjoy. Listen to your body's needs and give it the nourishment and movement it requires to thrive.

Celebrating Achievements

Acknowledge and celebrate your accomplishments, no matter how small they may seem. Recognize your efforts and the progress you have made along your personal journey. Treat yourself to something special or engage in activities that bring you a sense of fulfillment and joy when you achieve a goal or milestone.

Practicing Mindfulness

Cultivate mindfulness by bringing your attention to the present moment without judgment. Allow yourself to experience and accept your thoughts, emotions, and sensations as they arise, fostering a sense of self-awareness and compassion.

Here are a few ideas for practicing mindfulness and self-awareness:

- **Mindful Breathing.** Take a few moments each day to focus on your breath. Sit comfortably, close your eyes, and bring your attention to the sensation of your breath as it enters and leaves your body. Notice the rhythm, depth, and pace of your breath, allowing yourself to fully experience the present moment.
- **Body Scan Meditation.** Set aside dedicated time to practice a body scan meditation. Start from the top of your head and slowly move your attention down to different parts of your body, observing any sensations or tension you may notice. Allow yourself to fully embrace and accept these sensations without judgment or the need to change them.
- **Mindful Eating.** Engage in mindful eating by savoring each bite of your meals. Take the time to appreciate the colors, smells, textures, and flavors of your food. Chew slowly and pay attention to the sensations and tastes as you nourish your body. This practice enhances your connection with the present moment and cultivates gratitude for the nourishment you receive.
- **Daily Mindfulness Check-In.** Dedicate a few minutes each day to a mindfulness check-in. Sit in a quiet space and bring your attention to your thoughts, emotions, and sensations. Observe them without judgment, allowing them to arise and pass by like clouds in the sky. This practice fosters self-

awareness and helps you develop a compassionate and non-reactive stance towards your inner experiences.

- **Mindful Walking.** Engage in mindful walking by paying attention to the sensations of each step. Notice the contact of your feet with the ground, the movement of your legs, and the rhythm of your walk. Allow yourself to be fully present in the experience, tuning into the sights, sounds, and sensations around you.
- **Mindful Listening.** Practice mindful listening in your interactions with others. Give your full attention to whoever is speaking with you, without interrupting or formulating responses in your mind. Be present and truly listen, fostering deep connections and understanding.
- **Mindfulness in Daily Activities.** Bring mindfulness into everyday tasks such as washing dishes, brushing your teeth, or taking a shower. Instead of being on autopilot, bring your full attention to the sensations, movements, and actions involved in each activity. Engaging in these tasks mindfully can transform them into moments of self-care and presence.

Positive Self-Talk

Monitor your inner dialogue and replace self-critical thoughts with kind and supportive affirmations. Remind yourself of your strengths, accomplishments, and the progress you have made. Treat yourself with the same kindness and encouragement you would offer a close friend.

Here are some examples of replacing self-critical thoughts with kind and supportive affirmations:

Self-Critical Thought: "I always mess things up."

> Kind and Supportive Affirmation: "I am capable and resilient. I learn from my mistakes and grow stronger with each experience."

Self-Critical Thought: "I'm not good enough compared to others."

> Kind and Supportive Affirmation: "I embrace my unique qualities and celebrate my own journey. I am enough just as I am."

Self-Critical Thought: "I'll never be successful in my career."

> Kind and Supportive Affirmation: "I have the skills, determination, and potential to achieve my career goals. I am deserving of success and will keep working towards it."

Self-Critical Thought: "I always let people down."

> Kind and Supportive Affirmation: "I am considerate and caring towards others. I do my best, and sometimes things don't go as planned but it's okay. I am learning and growing every day."

Self-Critical Thought: "I'm not as talented as others."

Kind and Supportive Affirmation: "I have my own unique talents and strengths. I appreciate and nurture my abilities, and I am constantly evolving and improving."

Self-Critical Thought: "I don't deserve happiness."

Kind and Supportive Affirmation: "I am worthy of love, joy, and happiness. I deserve to prioritize my well-being and pursue a fulfilling and meaningful life."

Self-Critical Thought: "I'm a failure because I didn't reach my goal."

Kind and Supportive Affirmation: "Not reaching my goal doesn't define me. I celebrate my efforts and the progress I have made. I am resilient and will continue to pursue my dreams."

Self-Critical Thought: "I always make the wrong decisions."

Kind and Supportive Affirmation: "I trust my intuition and make decisions based on what I know at the time. I am open to learning and adjusting my path as needed."

Self-Critical Thought: "I'll never be confident."

Kind and Supportive Affirmation: "I am capable of building confidence within myself. I embrace my strengths and step out of my comfort zone to grow and develop."

Self-Critical Thought: "I'm not worthy of
love and acceptance."

> Kind and Supportive Affirmation: "I am
> deserving of love and acceptance, including
> my own. I treat myself with compassion and
> embrace my authentic self."

Surrounding Yourself with Positivity

Surround yourself with people who uplift and support
you. Create a positive and nurturing environment that aligns
with your values and aspirations. Engage in activities and
hobbies that bring you joy and foster positive emotions.

Here are a few ideas you can explore:

- Join a supportive community or group that shares
  your interests and values, such as a book club,
  sports team, volunteer organization, or online
  communities and forums.
- Pursue new or old hobbies that bring you joy and
  allow you to express your creativity, like painting,
  knitting, dancing, playing a musical instrument, or
  writing.
- Engage in physical activities that make you feel
  good, such as yoga, running, hiking, or playing a
  team sport. Regular exercise releases endorphins
  and promotes overall well-being.
- Attend events, workshops, or seminars related to
  your interests or personal development. These
  provide opportunities to connect with like-
  minded individuals who share similar passions.

- Seek out mentors or role models who have achieved success in areas that align with your goals. Their guidance and support can be invaluable.
- Schedule regular catch-ups or outings with friends who uplift and inspire you. Surrounding yourself with positive influences can enhance your overall well-being.
- Declutter and organize your physical space to create a sense of order and harmony. A clean and tidy environment can contribute to a positive mindset.
- Fill your living and working spaces with items that bring you joy, such as meaningful artwork, plants, sentimental objects, or motivational quotes and affirmations.
- Carve out time for self-care rituals, such as taking relaxing baths, practicing mindfulness or meditation, or indulging in activities that help you unwind and recharge.

Seeking Support

Remember that when you seek support, it is a sign of strength, not weakness. Reach out to trusted friends, family members, or professionals when you need guidance, encouragement, or assistance. Surround yourself with a network of support that understands and values your well-being.

* * *

The above are just a few practical examples of how you can incorporate self-love into your daily life. Remember that self-love is a journey and a practice that requires consistent effort and compassion. By prioritizing self-love, you empower yourself to live a more fulfilling and authentic life.

CHAPTER 7: LEVEL UP WITH KANBAN: A VISUAL TOOL FOR GETTING THINGS DONE

To-Do lists have long been a staple in our everyday lives in our effort to become productive and organized. They serve as a valuable tool for capturing tasks, setting priorities, and tracking progress. With the goal setting discussed earlier, we have to hit those objectives and to hit those objectives, we have to hit those smaller goals, which can be in our to-do lists every day that we're hitting on a daily basis.

In the pursuit of accomplishing our goals and objectives, effective task management plays a vital role, especially as our lives become increasingly complex and fast-paced. One valuable method for task organization and increased productivity is the Kanban system. Derived from the Japanese words "kan" meaning sign and "ban" meaning board, Kanban has a rich history rooted in signage to capture attention. Originally designed for team use, it has been adapted to suit individual task management needs.

The Kanban system is a tool that visually represents tasks and their progress. Its origins can be traced back to a

Japanese car manufacturer, Toyota, where it was initially introduced as a visual scheduling system. In 2007, the Kanban board was created, offering a basic framework consisting of three columns: "To Do," "In Progress," and "Complete." However, this system is fully customizable to meet individual preferences and requirements.

What makes the Kanban system effective? Firstly, it ensures that the right work happens at the right time. By visualizing tasks on the board, priorities become clear, allowing for better time allocation and task management. Understanding the workload and the tasks that need to be assigned becomes effortless. Secondly, it shifts the focus from simply starting work to finishing work. The emphasis is on the flow and progress of tasks, which encourages a sense of accomplishment and motivates individuals to complete their work.

One particularly useful variation of the Kanban system, which I learned from a workshop I attended during Mental Health Awareness Month in May 2023, incorporates three animal symbols: the frog, the Koi fish, and the woodpecker. While doing some research on this variation, I discovered that this is based on a desktop system/tool created by the company myKanban, but there are no other written resources that I could find about this variation. However, since I really liked the concepts I gathered and I find them useful, I want to take this opportunity to share them with you here in this book. Let's delve into each animal and its corresponding task column.

THE FROG

Have you ever found yourself leaving important tasks until the last minute? It's a common tendency we humans have. Sometimes, a seemingly small task can eat up most of our day, leaving us with little time for what truly matters. That's where the frog comes in. By picking the frog task—the top priority—first thing in the morning, you set a time limit to complete it. You'll be amazed at how much difference it makes to tackle one important piece of work every day.

The quote associated with the frog is, "Eat a live frog first thing in the morning, and nothing worse will happen to you the rest of the day." The frog represents top-priority tasks. Each morning, you select one crucial task and designate it as your frog. By focusing on completing this task early in the day, you create a sense of urgency and limit procrastination. Accomplishing an important task right away sets a positive tone for the rest of the day.

In fact, you can add two to three of these high-priority tasks in the frog column on your Kanban board. It's like giving yourself a roadmap to success right from the start.

THE KOI FISH

Next up, let's talk about the Koi fish. Koi means carp in Japanese, and it symbolizes perseverance. The Koi fish represents the idea of pushing against challenges and persevering in the face of obstacles. Just like the fish known for its ability to swim upstream and resist the flow of water, these tasks in the Kanban system represent your high-effort, high-reward items. These are the longer and more significant items on your to-do list that make up the bulk of your day.

When you identify and label your high-effort, high-reward tasks as Koi fish on your Kanban board, you bring attention to their significance and ensure that they receive the necessary focus and effort, and you become less likely to get distracted. It puts you in a proactive mindset and helps you stay focused on what truly matters.

Breaking down complex tasks into smaller subtasks is another valuable strategy that aligns with the Koi fish metaphor. Just as the Koi fish navigates the stream by taking one step (or tailfin!) at a time, dividing complex tasks into more manageable subtasks allows you to approach them with a sense of progress and achievement. It also helps prevent overwhelm and provides a clear roadmap for completing the larger task.

The Koi fish column captures these middle-priority tasks, which are important but may not require the same level of immediate attention as the high-priority ones. Allocating tasks to this space gives them the necessary focus without overshadowing the urgency of the high-priority items.

THE WOODPECKER

Now, let's not forget the woodpecker. Picture this bird tapping away at a thousand trees, but accomplishing nothing. However, when it focuses its effort on one tree, it eventually finds dinner. Similarly, the woodpecker column on your Kanban board represents your low-priority tasks. In today's hyper-connected world, we can easily get caught up in responding to every notification or engaging in tasks that seem urgent but aren't truly important. They can easily consume your entire workday if you're not disciplined.

These "woodpecker" tasks, while urgent, are low in

importance compared to others. It is crucial to recognize these tasks and allocate time for them appropriately.

Think of them as the $10 tasks, not the $10,000 ones. Writing numerous woodpecker tasks down may give us a quick dopamine hit when we check them off, but it's a cardinal sin in productivity. If we keep focusing on these small, insignificant tasks, we'll realize that our more important work isn't getting done.

By designating specific times, such as natural pauses in the day, to address woodpecker tasks, you prevent them from overshadowing more important work. Remember, it is essential to distinguish between small, low-value tasks and those that truly contribute to significant progress. By doing so, you can maintain focus on your frog and koi fish tasks while still addressing the woodpecker tasks when appropriate.

CLASSIFYING TASKS

Here are some examples of how the Kanban method can be applied using the concepts of the frog, Koi fish, and woodpecker:

Frog

- For example, if you have an important client presentation due at the end of the week, it becomes your frog task. You would focus your energy and resources on completing this task first, ensuring that it receives the attention it deserves and is completed in a timely manner.

- A marketing manager has a product launch scheduled for next month. The creation of promotional materials, coordinating with the design team, and finalizing the marketing strategy would be the frog tasks in this case.
- A student has an upcoming exam in a week. Studying for the exam, completing assignments, and reviewing lecture notes would be the frog tasks that require immediate attention.
- A project manager has a critical client meeting scheduled for tomorrow. Preparing the presentation, gathering relevant data, and finalizing the agenda would be the frog tasks that require immediate attention.
- A freelance designer has a tight deadline for a client's website redesign project. Creating the wireframes, designing the homepage, and optimizing the user interface would be the frog tasks in this case.

Koi Fish

- Let's say you are working on a long-term project that requires various research and analysis tasks. These tasks are crucial for the success of the project but may not have tight deadlines. By creating a Koi fish column on your Kanban board, you can capture and track these tasks, ensuring they receive the necessary attention while still maintaining focus on the urgent frog tasks.
- A software development team has ongoing feature enhancements for a product. While the

development of critical bug fixes and resolving technical issues would be the frog tasks, working on the planned feature enhancements without immediate deadlines would fall into the Koi fish category.

- A homeowner has a home improvement project with a long-term deadline. The major renovations, such as repairing the roof or fixing plumbing issues, would be the frog tasks, while smaller tasks like repainting the walls or replacing light fixtures would be the Koi fish tasks.

- A business owner is working on expanding their product line. Researching potential suppliers, evaluating manufacturing costs, and conducting market analysis would be the Koi fish tasks that contribute to the long-term growth of the business.

- A student is planning a study abroad program for the next year. Researching different destinations, exploring scholarship opportunities, and preparing the required documentation would fall into the Koi fish category as they require careful consideration but are not immediately time-sensitive.

Woodpecker

- Let's say you want to learn a new language. You decide to allocate 30 minutes every day to practice vocabulary, grammar, and pronunciation. This daily practice, represented by the woodpecker, helps you make steady progress and develop your language skills over time.

- A writer aims to complete a novel. Setting aside a specific time each day for writing, whether it's 30 minutes or an hour, represents the woodpecker concept. Consistently chipping away at the writing tasks helps the writer make progress towards completing the book.
- An entrepreneur wants to improve their public speaking skills. Practicing public speaking techniques for a few minutes every day, such as rehearsing a speech or delivering a short presentation, reflects the woodpecker concept. These small but regular efforts contribute to their overall growth and development in public speaking.
- A fitness enthusiast wants to improve their strength. Incorporating a short strength training routine into their daily workout, focusing on specific muscle groups each day, exemplifies the woodpecker concept. Consistent effort over time helps them gradually build strength.
- An aspiring musician aims to learn a new instrument. Practicing scales, learning new chords, and playing short pieces regularly, even for a few minutes each day, represents the woodpecker concept. The cumulative effect of consistent practice leads to significant progress over time.

With the above examples, I hope these give you a better idea of how to classify your tasks depending on your individual circumstances and goals. The key is to identify the most urgent and important tasks (frog), the important but less urgent tasks (Koi fish), and the small, consistent efforts for continuous improvement (woodpecker) in your specific context to effectively apply the Kanban method and enhance productivity.

* * *

By embracing Kanban and incorporating the frog, Koi fish, and woodpecker method into your daily life, you can enhance your sense of organization and overall productivity. This visual approach encourages prioritization, focus, and a sense of accomplishment as tasks move across the board. It helps combat procrastination, keeps you on track to achieve your goals, and make the most out of each day.

When you revamp your task management with the Kanban system, you will be able to experience the benefits of visual organization, increased productivity, and a greater sense of accomplishment as you progress towards your goals.

CHAPTER 8: BUILDING RESILIENCE AND SELF-KINDNESS

Resilience is a fundamental quality that enables individuals to navigate the challenges and setbacks they encounter in life. It is the ability to bounce back from adversity, adapt to change, and maintain a positive outlook despite difficult circumstances. Building resilience goes hand in hand with cultivating self-kindness, as it provides the foundation for a compassionate and supportive relationship with oneself. By understanding the role of resilience in self-kindness, you can develop the inner strength and compassion needed to navigate life's ups and downs.

Resilience is not an innate trait but a skill that can be learned and cultivated. It involves developing a mindset and adopting strategies that foster adaptability, emotional well-being, and perseverance. Resilience allows you to confront and overcome challenges, setbacks, and even trauma, without losing hope or becoming overwhelmed. It is an empowering quality that enables you to maintain a sense of agency and control over your life, even in the face of adversity.

Resilience and self-kindness are closely intertwined. Resilience provides the inner strength and capacity to respond to adversity with self-compassion and understanding. When you have the ability to acknowledge your struggles and setbacks without self-judgment or self-blame, that is resilience. It is not about being invincible or unaffected by challenges but rather about embracing your humanness and treating yourself with kindness and care.

DEVELOPING RESILIENCE SKILLS

Developing resilience skills is essential for you to effectively navigate the inevitable challenges, setbacks, and uncertainties that arise in life. We will explore some key resilience skills along with examples to illustrate their practical application in real-life situations.

Positive Self-Beliefs

Developing positive self-beliefs is a foundational resilience skill. It involves cultivating a sense of self-worth, confidence, and optimism. By fostering a positive belief in your abilities, you are able face challenges with resilience and perseverance.

Let's take this example of Matthew. Matthew is a college student in his final year who receives a lower grade than expected on an important exam. Instead of internalizing the setback as a reflection of his intelligence, being the resilient person that he is with positive self-beliefs, he recognized the grade as a temporary setback and believes in his ability to improve through further effort and learning, especially as he's already reached his final year in college, and is close to the finish line in this stage of his life.

Flexibility and Adaptability

Flexibility and adaptability are important resilience skills that enable you to adjust and respond effectively to changing circumstances. Being open-minded, embracing change, and finding alternative solutions when faced with obstacles are essential aspects of this skill.

Let's take this next example of Andy. Andy is a project coordinator of 10 years at an engineering company. He gets called into a meeting with the operations manager one day and is told that he is being let go. With the news of his unexpected job loss, he may initially feel discouraged. However, by maintaining a flexible mindset, he viewed this as an opportunity for career exploration and personal growth. He was able to consider alternative career paths, engage in networking, and acquire new skills to enhance his employability. Because of his flexibility and adaptability, he eventually landed a new job as a managing director at an IT consulting firm.

Problem-Solving and Decision-Making

Resilience is closely linked to problem-solving and decision-making skills. Being able to analyze situations, identify potential solutions, and make informed decisions contributes to effective problem-solving, even in challenging circumstances.

For this example, we have Kathy. Kathy is a small business owner who faces a significant setback when her main supplier suddenly goes out of business. Instead of becoming overwhelmed, she draws on her problem-solving skills. She researches alternative suppliers and fortunately, she found one in the next town over. At the same time, she went on to negotiate new contracts with her other existing suppliers after finding the presence of similar suppliers. She also explored new approaches to ensure the continuity of her business operations.

Emotion Regulation

Emotion regulation is an essential resilience skill that involves recognizing, understanding, and managing your emotions in a healthy and constructive manner. It enables you to maintain emotional balance, cope with stress, and make rational decisions during challenging times.

Let's look at this example of Linda. Linda is the caregiver of a family member with a chronic illness. As the caregiving responsibility falls mainly on her, she may experience intense emotions such as frustration, sadness, or guilt. It was never easy for her at the beginning, but through the development of emotion regulation skills, she was able to acknowledge and validate her emotions while seeking healthy coping strategies, such as engaging in self-care activities, seeking support from her extended family and friends, and practicing mindfulness techniques.

Optimism and Gratitude

Cultivating optimism and gratitude is a resilience skill that involves adopting a positive outlook and appreciating the positive aspects of life, even in challenging circumstances. By focusing on the good and practicing gratitude, you can maintain hope and resilience in the face of adversity.

As an example, a person facing financial difficulties may consciously practice optimism and gratitude by reflecting on the things they still have, such as supportive relationships, good health, or personal strengths. This is sometimes easier said than done. The important thing to keep in mind is that by shifting your focus to the positives, you can maintain resilience and approach challenges with a sense of gratitude for what you do have.

* * *

In addition to the above resilience skills, building and maintaining a strong support network is also crucial. Having trusted friends, family members, or mentors who provide emotional support, encouragement, and practical assistance can significantly enhance resilience in times of adversity.

To give an example, divorce is never easy. For a person going through this unfortunate situation, they are able to rely on the support of close friends and family members. These individuals offer a listening ear, provide reassurance, and help with practical matters such as childcare or finding legal guidance. The presence of a supportive network strengthens resilience and promotes a sense of belonging and connectedness.

I recognize that some people do not have the luxury of having an easily accessible support network. If you are in this position, remember that you are not alone in your struggles. There are some online groups or there could be some local community groups in your area where you can find support, so I encourage you to seek these groups and when you are able, to offer support to others in return as well.

Developing resilience skills is a continuous process that empowers you to navigate life's challenges with strength, adaptability, and self-compassion. By cultivating positive self-beliefs, flexibility, problem-solving abilities, emotion regulation, optimism, and gratitude, and having social support, individuals can enhance their resilience and effectively cope with adversity. These skills are not innate but can be developed through practice and self-reflection. By actively engaging in resilience-building activities and seeking support when needed, individuals can build inner strength and foster self-kindness, leading to greater well-being and success in all areas of life.

OVERCOMING SETBACKS AND CHALLENGES WITH SELF-KINDNESS

During challenging times, practicing self-kindness becomes important for building resilience. It involves being gentle and compassionate with yourself, acknowledging emotions, and providing comfort and support. Self-kindness gives you permission to rest, recover, and seek help when needed. It promotes a nurturing inner dialogue, where self-criticism is replaced with self-acceptance and self-encouragement.

Resilience and self-kindness enable you to embrace failure as a natural part of the growth process. Rather than viewing failures as reflections of personal shortcomings, individuals with resilience and self-kindness approach them as valuable learning opportunities. They recognize that setbacks and mistakes are opportunities for growth, and they respond with self-compassion, seeking lessons and insights that can contribute to their personal development.

So when you are faced with setbacks and challenges, be kind to yourself as you overcome adversity and maintain your resilience. Approach it with curiosity and a willingness to learn. Here are some strategies for overcoming setbacks and challenges with self-kindness:

Acknowledge and Validate Emotions

Self-kindness begins with acknowledging and validating your emotions. It is normal to feel disappointed, frustrated, or upset when faced with setbacks or challenges. Instead of suppressing or ignoring these emotions, allow yourself to experience them fully. Recognize that it is okay to feel a range of emotions and give yourself permission to process them in a healthy and supportive manner.

For example, if you experience a setback in your career such as not getting the promotion that you worked hard for, you may feel a sense of disappointment and self-doubt. Instead of berating yourself for not achieving that goal, practice self-kindness by acknowledging and accepting your emotions. Allow yourself to grieve the loss, and then shift your focus towards finding solutions and moving forward.

Practice Compassionate Self-Talk

The way you talk to yourself during difficult times can greatly impact your resilience and well-being. Instead of engaging in self-critical or negative self-talk, cultivate self-compassionate self-talk. Treat yourself with the same kindness and understanding you would offer to a friend in a similar situation.

For instance, if you make a mistake or face a setback, instead of berating yourself with thoughts like "I'm such a failure" or "I'll never get it right," practice self-kindness by reframing your self-talk. Replace self-criticism with self-compassionate statements such as "It's okay to make mistakes; they are opportunities for growth" or "I am doing my best, and I will learn from this experience."

Practice Self-Care

Self-kindness involves prioritizing your well-being and practicing self-care. Taking care of your physical, emotional, and mental health is crucial for building resilience and bouncing back from setbacks. Engage in activities that nurture and recharge you, such as exercising, getting enough sleep, eating nourishing food, practicing relaxation techniques, or engaging in hobbies that bring you joy.

Self-care also means setting boundaries and knowing when to rest and recharge. Pushing yourself excessively without allowing time for rest and self-care can deplete your resilience. Remember that self-kindness includes giving yourself permission to take breaks, say no when needed, and prioritize your well-being.

* * *

Overcoming setbacks and challenges with self-kindness is a powerful way to build resilience and maintain well-being. By acknowledging and validating your emotions, practicing self-compassionate self-talk, seeking support, and prioritizing self-care, you can navigate difficult times with grace and bounce back stronger. Remember that setbacks and challenges are not indicative of your worth or abilities. With self-kindness as your compass, you can cultivate resilience and thrive in the face of adversity.

CULTIVATING A RESILIENT MINDSET

In the pursuit of personal growth and navigating life's challenges, cultivating a resilient mindset is essential. Self-care is an essential aspect of having a resilient mindset. Taking care of your physical, emotional, and mental well-being helps you recharge and maintain your inner resources. Engaging in activities that bring joy, practicing mindfulness, maintaining healthy relationships, and setting boundaries are all examples of self-care practices that contribute to building resilience and fostering self-kindness. By prioritizing self-care, you enhance your capacity to handle challenges and cultivate a compassionate relationship with yourself.

Physical self-care is about nourishing the body and prioritizing its well-being. This can involve engaging in regular exercise, maintaining a balanced and nutritious diet, getting enough sleep, and attending to one's physical health needs. Taking care of the body not only enhances physical resilience but also contributes to improved mental and emotional well-being.

Emotional self-care involves recognizing and honoring one's emotions and processing them in a healthy and constructive way. It is essential to develop emotional awareness and cultivate healthy coping mechanisms for dealing with difficult emotions. This can include practices such as journaling, engaging in creative outlets, seeking emotional support from loved ones or therapists, and engaging in activities that bring emotional fulfillment.

Mental self-care focuses on nurturing the mind and promoting mental well-being. This can involve engaging in activities that stimulate the mind, such as reading, learning new skills, solving puzzles, or engaging in hobbies that promote mental agility. Additionally, practicing mindfulness and meditation can help you cultivate present-moment awareness, stay focused, adaptable, and develop a more resilient mindset.

Social self-care emphasizes the importance of healthy relationships, boundaries, and connections with others. Building a support network of trusted friends, family, or mentors provides a sense of belonging and support during difficult times. Engaging in meaningful and fulfilling relationships nurtures emotional well-being and provides a source of encouragement and perspective.

Practicing self-compassion is another key component of cultivating a resilient mindset. Self-compassion involves treating yourself with kindness, understanding, and acceptance in times of difficulty or failure. It means acknowledging your imperfections and mistakes without harsh self-judgment. When faced with setbacks or challenges, offer yourself the same care and support you would extend to a dear friend. With self-compassion, you are allowed to learn from your mistakes, bounce back from failures, and maintain a positive and nurturing inner dialogue. Keep in mind that setbacks are temporary, while effort and perseverance are essential ingredients for success. Embrace challenges, seek feedback, and be open to new strategies and approaches.

Remember, developing a resilient mindset is an ongoing

process that requires practice, and a commitment to personal growth.

* * *

U nderstanding resilience and its role in self-kindness is essential for personal growth, well-being, and navigating life's challenges. Resilience allows you to bounce back from adversity, while self-kindness provides the nurturing and compassionate mindset needed to face challenges with self-compassion and understanding. By building resilience and practicing self-kindness, you develop the inner strength and compassion required to thrive in the face of adversity and cultivate a positive relationship with yourself. Embracing resilience and self-kindness as lifelong practices empowers you to embrace your journey, celebrate your progress, and approach life's ups and downs with self-acceptance.

CHAPTER 9: SELF-REFLECTION AND GROWTH

THE POWER OF SELF-REFLECTION

Self-reflection is a powerful tool for personal growth and development. It is the process of examining your thoughts, emotions, and actions in a conscious and introspective manner. You gain insights into yourself, your experiences, and your relationships, leading to a deeper understanding of who you are and how you can grow.

The power of self-reflection lies in its ability to bring awareness to your thoughts, beliefs, and behaviors. It allows you to pause, step back, and observe yourself from a more objective perspective. By taking the time to reflect, you create a space for self-awareness and self-discovery, enabling you to make intentional choices and take proactive steps towards personal growth.

Self-reflection provides an opportunity to examine your values, beliefs, and goals. It helps you align your actions with your core values and identify any areas of incongruence. For example, through self-reflection, you may realize that you have been prioritizing work over your well-being or neglecting your relationships. Recognizing these misalignments allows you to make necessary adjustments and live a more authentic and fulfilling life.

Moreover, self-reflection helps you gain a deeper understanding of your emotions and triggers. It allows you to explore the underlying causes of your emotional reactions and patterns of behavior. For instance, if you find yourself consistently feeling anxious in social situations, self-reflection can help you uncover the triggers, the root causes of this anxiety, such as fear of judgment or a lack of self-confidence. With this understanding, you can develop strategies to manage your emotions and overcome these challenges.

Self-reflection also promotes self-accountability. It encourages you to take responsibility for your choices and actions. Through honest self-assessment, you can acknowledge areas where you may have fallen short or made mistakes. This process of self-accountability fosters personal growth and empowers you to make positive changes in your life. After all, you are the best person who knows yourself.

In addition, self-reflection enhances your problem-solving and decision-making abilities. By reflecting on past experiences and outcomes, you can identify patterns and learn from both your successes and failures. You can assess the effectiveness of our strategies and make adjustments for future endeavors. Self-reflection allows you to tap into your wisdom and apply your insights to navigate challenges more effectively.

Furthermore, self-reflection strengthens your self-compassion. It enables you to practice self-acceptance and understanding, recognizing that you are a human being with strengths and limitations. Through self-reflection, you can cultivate a more compassionate inner dialogue, replacing self-judgment with self-encouragement.

Self-reflection can take various forms depending on your individual preferences and needs. Some people find journaling to be an effective way to reflect, allowing them to express their thoughts and emotions freely. Others may prefer meditation or mindfulness practices that provide a calm and focused space for self-exploration. Engaging in meaningful conversations with trusted friends or seeking professional guidance through therapy or coaching can also facilitate deep self-reflection.

To make the most of self-reflection, it is essential that you create dedicated time and space for introspection. Setting aside regular periods for self-reflection, whether it's daily, weekly, or monthly, helps establish a habit and ensures that you prioritize this valuable practice. Finding a quiet and comfortable environment where you can focus without distractions can further enhance the depth of your self-reflection.

RECOGNIZING AREAS FOR PERSONAL GROWTH

Recognizing areas for personal growth is a vital aspect of self-reflection and a catalyst for personal development. It involves acknowledging areas of your life where you have the potential to grow, improve, and expand your capabilities. By identifying these areas, you open yourself up to new opportunities, enhance your skills, and create a path towards self-fulfillment and self-actualization.

One of the first steps in recognizing areas for personal growth is self-awareness. It is about becoming attuned to your strengths, weaknesses, interests, and aspirations. Self-awareness allows you to gain insight into who you are, your values, and what truly matters to you. You can examine your thoughts, emotions, and behaviors to uncover patterns, strengths, and areas where you may need further development.

Self-awareness also involves understanding the impact of your actions and choices on yourself and others. By recognizing the consequences of your behavior, you can identify areas where you can improve your interactions, communication skills, and relationships. For example, if you notice that you tend to be impatient or quick to judge, self-awareness prompts you to work on developing qualities such as empathy, active listening, and open-mindedness.

Recognizing areas for personal growth also requires self-reflection on your goals and aspirations. By assessing where you currently are in relation to where you want to be, you can identify the gaps and areas that need improvement. This involves clarifying your values and setting meaningful goals that align with your vision for yourself. For example, if you aspire to become more physically fit, you may recognize the need to improve your exercise routine, nutrition habits, or mindset around fitness.

It is important to approach the process of recognizing areas for personal growth with self-compassion. Instead of viewing your shortcomings as flaws or failures, you can choose to see them as opportunities for growth and development.

One way to identify areas for personal growth is by seeking feedback from trusted sources. Feedback from mentors, colleagues, friends, or family members can provide valuable insights into areas where you may be blind to your own limitations or opportunities. Constructive feedback allows you to gain different perspectives, challenge your assumptions, and identify areas where you can develop new skills or refine existing ones.

Self-awareness also involves exploring your passions and interests. By engaging in activities that bring you joy and fulfillment, you can uncover new talents or discover untapped potential. Exploring new hobbies, taking on challenging projects, or pursuing further education or training in areas of interest can open doors to personal growth and self-discovery.

In recognizing areas for personal growth, it is important to set realistic and achievable goals. Break down larger goals into smaller, manageable steps that can be measured and tracked. This allows you to celebrate progress along the way and maintain motivation. By setting specific goals, you create a roadmap for personal growth and ensure that your efforts are focused and purposeful.

CULTIVATING A GROWTH MINDSET

Cultivating a growth mindset is a powerful tool for personal growth and development. It is the belief that your abilities, intelligence, and qualities can be developed through dedication, effort, and continuous learning. With a growth mindset, you embrace challenges, persist in the face of setbacks, and view failures as opportunities for growth. This mindset fosters resilience, creativity, and a passion for learning, enabling you to reach new heights of achievement and personal fulfillment.

One of the key aspects of cultivating a growth mindset is the understanding that your potential is not fixed. You are not limited by your current abilities or circumstances.

Instead, you have the capacity to learn, adapt, and improve throughout your life. This belief empowers you to take on new challenges and step outside of your comfort zone, knowing that with effort and perseverance, you can develop new skills and overcome obstacles.

Cultivating a growth mindset begins with the language you use to describe yourself and your abilities. It involves reframing negative self-talk and transforming it into positive, growth-oriented statements. Instead of saying, "I'm not good at this," you can shift your mindset to, "I haven't mastered this yet, but I'm willing to put in the effort to improve." By changing your internal dialogue, you create a more empowering narrative that fuels your motivation and resilience. You can refer back to Chapter 3 where I talked about replacing negative thoughts with positive ones and Chapter 6 where I shared examples of positive self-talk.

Another important aspect of cultivating a growth mindset is embracing challenges. Rather than shying away from difficulties, you need to actively seek them out as opportunities for growth. Challenges provide the chance to stretch your abilities, learn new skills, and expand your knowledge. They push you outside of your comfort zone and stimulate your brain's capacity for adaptation and growth. By embracing challenges, you develop resilience, perseverance, and a sense of achievement as you overcome obstacles and reach new levels of mastery.

Effort and perseverance are central to the cultivation of a growth mindset. True growth and improvement require sustained effort and dedication. With a growth mindset, you would approach setbacks with resilience and view them as stepping stones on the path to success.

Cultivating a growth mindset also involves seeking out

inspiration and learning from others. You should recognize that there is much to be gained from the wisdom and experiences of those who have achieved success in your areas of interest. Engage in conversations, read books, attend workshops, or seek mentors who can provide guidance and support. By surrounding yourself with individuals who embody a growth mindset, you create a positive and motivating environment that will encourage you to strive for continuous improvement.

In addition to seeking external sources of inspiration, cultivating a growth mindset also requires self-reflection and self-awareness as we've already discussed. Take the time to identify your strengths, weaknesses, and areas for growth.

A growth mindset is not only beneficial for personal growth but also for fostering positive relationships and collaboration. When you believe that others can grow and develop, you are more likely to support and encourage their efforts. You can celebrate their successes and offer constructive feedback to help them improve. By fostering a growth mindset in your interactions with others, you create an environment that promotes collective learning, collaboration, and innovation.

Cultivating a growth mindset is an ongoing process. It requires patience, persistence, and a commitment to lifelong learning. It is about approaching every experience with an open mind and a willingness to grow. By embracing challenges, putting in effort, seeking inspiration, and reflecting on your progress, you can continue to develop and evolve, unlocking your full potential and leading a life of continuous growth and personal fulfillment.

EMBRACING MISTAKES AND LEARNING FROM FAILURE

Embracing mistakes and learning from failure is a crucial aspect of self-reflection and personal growth. Rather than fearing or avoiding failures, you can choose to see them as valuable opportunities for learning, growth, and resilience. When you embrace your mistakes and failures, you cultivate a mindset that encourages continuous improvement, innovation, and the development of your full potential.

Mistakes and failures are inevitable parts of the human experience. No matter how skilled or knowledgeable you are, you will encounter setbacks and make errors along your journey. However, it is your response to these setbacks that determines your growth and progress. By embracing your mistakes, you shift your perspective from seeing them as evidence of your shortcomings to viewing them as stepping stones on the path to success.

Instead of seeing failure as a negative reflection of your abilities or worth, you can view it as a natural part of the learning process. Failure provides you with valuable feedback and insights into what works and what doesn't. It highlights areas where you can improve, adjust your strategies, and develop new skills. Reframing failure as a learning opportunity allows you to create a more positive and constructive approach to setbacks.

Embracing mistakes and learning from failure requires self-compassion. Rather than being overly critical or judgmental towards yourself, you need to bring kindness and understanding, without falling into a cycle of self-blame or shame. With self-compassion, you create an environment of psychological safety that encourages risk-taking and growth.

When you take the time to reflect on what went wrong, what could have been done differently, and what lessons can be gleaned from the experience, it allows you to extract valuable insights. Reflective practices, such as journaling or engaging in meaningful conversations with trusted individuals, provide opportunities to gain clarity and deepen our understanding of the situation. Through reflection, you can identify patterns, strengths, and areas for improvement, guiding your future actions and decision-making.

Learning from failure also involves embracing resilience and persistence. Setbacks can be discouraging and demotivating, but by developing resilience, you bounce back stronger and more determined. Setbacks and failures are not permanent states but temporary obstacles on your path to success. They make you better equipped to face future failures with a sense of perseverance and optimism.

With a growth mindset, failures are opportunities for growth and improvement. You embrace challenges, persist in the face of setbacks, and view feedback as valuable information for learning and progress.

Learning from failure is not solely an individual journey. It is also important to create an environment that supports and encourages learning from mistakes. In personal relationships, educational institutions, and workplaces, fostering a culture of psychological safety allows individuals to take risks, share their failures, and learn from each other's experiences. When mistakes are seen as opportunities for growth rather than reasons for punishment or judgment, individuals feel more comfortable being vulnerable, seeking feedback, and engaging in open dialogue.

SHARING THE LOVE

As you know, self-love is about embracing and accepting yourself, recognizing your worth, and nurturing your well-being. It's about cultivating a positive and compassionate relationship with yourself. And here's the thing: leaving a review is not just an opportunity to share your thoughts with others; it's also an act of self-love.

By the simple gesture of leaving your honest opinion of this book on Amazon and/or Goodreads, you are not only supporting me and my work as an author but also honoring your own experience and perspective. By sharing your thoughts and insights, you are validating your own voice and the value of your opinion to influence others, help them discover ideas and guidance, and spread love and learnings with them.

In addition, leaving a review is also an act of kindness. It helps fellow readers make an informed decision about my book, allowing them to discover narratives that may resonate with their own lives.

Thank you for your help. Love, knowledge, and positivity thrive when you share your enthusiasm, positive insights and experiences – and you're helping me share that gift with others!

SCAN THE QR CODE TO LEAVE A REVIEW

THE SELF-LOVE PATH

CONCLUSION

In the journey of personal growth and achievement, self-love and self-compassion are essential companions. Throughout this book, we have explored the significance of embracing self-compassion and kindness towards yourself as a powerful catalyst for personal transformation and goal attainment. By understanding and cultivating these qualities, you can navigate life's challenges with resilience, nurture your well-being, and unlock your true potential.

Self-love is not a selfish or narcissistic pursuit, but rather a deep acknowledgment and acceptance of your intrinsic worth and humanity. It is about treating yourself with the same compassion and kindness that we readily extend to others. By embracing self-love, you create a foundation of self-care that supports your overall well-being and enables you to show up fully in your life.

One of the core aspects of self-love is self-compassion, which involves recognizing your human experience of imperfection, vulnerability, and suffering. Through self-compassion, you learn to hold space for your own struggles, extend understanding and forgiveness to yourself, and cultivate a sense of psychological safety that fosters growth and resilience. This practice allows you to navigate setbacks, failures, and challenges with greater grace and adaptability.

By incorporating self-compassion into your daily life, you free yourself from the constraints of self-criticism and judgment. You learn to treat yourself with kindness, understanding that mistakes and missteps are natural and valuable opportunities for growth and learning. Self-compassion helps you break free from the cycle of negative self-talk and self-sabotaging behaviors, empowering you to make conscious choices aligned with your goals and values.

I've shared with you various practical strategies and tools for cultivating self-love and self-compassion, which you can continue to explore daily. We have discussed the importance of mindfulness and self-awareness in recognizing your thoughts, emotions, and inner narratives. By developing a non-judgmental and compassionate stance towards yourself, you can disentangle from negative patterns and cultivate a more positive and supportive inner dialogue.

When you truly love and accept yourself, you become more aligned with your authentic desires and aspirations. You gain clarity about your values, priorities, and the actions necessary to create a fulfilling life. Self-love allows you to set boundaries, make self-honoring choices, and pursue goals that resonate with your true self.

What's more, self-love and self-compassion have a ripple effect on your relationships and interactions with others. When you are kind and compassionate towards yourself, you are better equipped to extend the same qualities to those around you. This creates a positive and nurturing environment where empathy, understanding, and genuine connections thrive. By embracing self-love, we become a source of inspiration and encouragement for others to embark on their own self-discovery and personal growth journeys.

However, it is important to acknowledge that the path of self-love and self-compassion is not always linear or easy. It requires consistent practice, self-reflection, and a willingness to confront your inner fears and insecurities. There may be moments of resistance, setbacks, and self-doubt along the way. Yet, it is precisely in these moments that our commitment to self-love and self-compassion becomes most vital.

As we conclude this book, it is essential to remember that self-love and self-compassion are lifelong journeys. They are not destinations to be reached but rather ongoing practices to be cultivated and nurtured. Each day offers us opportunities to deepen our self-understanding, expand our capacity for kindness, and embrace our authentic selves more fully.

So, as you go on your own self-love path, remember to be patient and gentle with yourself. Celebrate your progress, no matter how small, and embrace the lessons and growth that come with each experience. Surround yourself with a supportive community and seek out resources that inspire and uplift you on your journey.

Ultimately, embracing self-love and self-compassion is a commitment to live authentically, love unconditionally, and create a life that reflects our truest desires and aspirations. By walking this path, you unleash your inner potential, foster well-being, and become catalysts for positive change.

May your self-love journey be filled with kindness, courage, and boundless possibilities. Remember, you are worthy of love, and your journey towards self-compassion is a testament to your strength and resilience. Trust in yourself, believe in your worth, and never forget to love yourself, for it is in this love that you will find the keys to unlocking your true potential.

FREE GIFT FOR MY READERS

Just for you! Get this free ebook as my gift to you for being my valued reader. You will have access to 5 weeks' worth of journal prompts (a total of 35) which serve as your invitation to explore different aspects of your journey on the self-love path, encouraging deep self-reflection and nurturing a positive mindset.

Visit ebook.arianeturpin.com/selflovejournal or scan the above QR code.

ABOUT THE AUTHOR

Ariane S. Turpin writes about love, relationships, and family. Before she started her book-writing journey, she maintained a personal blog and wrote articles for her school paper in her younger days. Her personal experiences of love and heartbreak from her long-term relationships and pseudo-relationships, before marrying the love of her life in her 30s, as well as the wealth of learnings she has accumulated over the years are what inspired her to carry on this path. Her hope is that her books will help you be the best person you can be, and you can be with the best person for you.

She is an advocate for diversity and inclusion, and wants readers from various backgrounds to be able to relate to her books and find inspiration. When she's not writing, she loves to explore the outdoors and workout.

Visit Ariane's website to find out more about her upcoming books at www.arianeturpin.com .

facebook.com/arianeturpinauthor
twitter.com/arianeturpincom
instagram.com/arianeturpinauthor
tiktok.com/@arianeturpinauthor

ALSO BY ARIANE S. TURPIN

Discover practical, proven strategies for creating and maintaining a loving, healthy partnership. Navigate better the inevitable challenges that arise in any relationship, even if you think everything is already common sense. Whether you're single and looking for love, or already in a relationship and seeking to improve it, create a life-changing partnership that lasts a lifetime from today!

Available on Amazon in Kindle edition, Paperback, and Hardcover.

https://www.amazon.com/stores/author/
B0C2VYNYT7

REFERENCES

Ackerman, Courtney, M.A. (2018, July 20). *What Is Self-Compassion and What Is Self-Love?* Positive Psychology. https://positivepsychology.com/self-compassion-self-love/

Borenstein, Jeffrey, M.D. (2020, February 12). *Self-Love and What It Means.* Brain & Behavior Research Foundation. https://www.bbrfoundation.org/blog/self-love-and-what-it-means

Clear, J. (n.d.). *Goal Setting: A Scientific Guide to Setting and Achieving Goals.* https://jamesclear.com/goal-setting

David, Susan. (2020, February 21). *How to be kinder to yourself.* https://ideas.ted.com/how-to-be-kinder-to-yourself-self-compassion/

Halton, Clay. (2022, September 28). *What Is the Kanban System?* Investopedia. https://www.investopedia.com/terms/k/kanban.asp

kanban tool. (n.d.) *History of Kanban.* https://kanbantool.com/kanban-guide/kanban-history

Kanbanize. (n.d) *What Is a Kanban Board and How to Use It? Basics Explained.* https://kanbanize.com/kanban-resources/getting-started/what-is-kanban-board

Martin, Sharon. (2020, April 23). *7 Types of Boundaries You May Need.* Psych-Central. https://psychcentral.com/blog/imperfect/2020/04/7-types-of-boundaries-you-may-need

Mind Tools. (n.d.) *Leap Forward With Backward Goal-Setting!* https://www.mindtools.com/actal93/leap-forward-with-backward-goal-setting

Mind Tools. (n.d.). *SMART Goals: How to Make Your Goals Achievable.* https://www.mindtools.com/a4wo118/smart-goals

Mind Tools. (n.d.) *The GROW Model of Coaching and Mentoring.* https://www.mindtools.com/an0fzpz/the-grow-model-of-coaching-and-mentoring

Moore, Catherine. (2019, June 2). *How to Practice Self-Compassion: 8 Techniques and Tips.* Positive Psychology. https://positivepsychology.com/how-to-practice-self-compassion

Murakamy. (n.d.) *The OKR Model – Leadership with Objectives and Key Results.* https://www.okracademy.com/okr-model

myKanban. (n.d.) https://www.mykanban.tech/

Neff, Kristin, Ph.D. (n.d.) *Research Publications.* Self-Compassion. https://self-compassion.org/the-research/

Pace, Karen. (2016, October 28). *Research shows that practicing self-compassion increases motivation.* Michigan State University Extension. https://www.canr.msu.edu/news/research_shows_that_practicing_self_compassion_increases_motivation

Scott, Elizabeth, Ph.D. (2022, May 24). *Negative Self-Talk and How It Affects Us.* Verywell Mind. https://www.verywellmind.com/negative-self-talk-and-how-it-affects-us-4161304

WOOP. (n.d.) *How can I practice WOOP?* WOOP. https://woopmylife.org/en/practice

Yop & Tom. (n.d.) *How To Plan & Achieve Your Goals (With The Power Of 3 Method).* https://www.yopandtom.com/blogs/news/how-to-plan-with-power-of-three

Printed in Great Britain
by Amazon

28561461R00096